[DAY 0

[DAY 1]

[DAY 2]

[DAY 3]

[DAY 7]

[DAY 8]

[DAY 9]

[DAY 10]

[DAY 11]

[DAY 14]

[DAY 15]

[DAY 16]

[DAY 17]

[DAY 18]

[DAY 21]

[DAY 22]

[DAY 23]

[DAY 24]

[DAY 25]

[DAY 28]

[DAY 29]

[DAY 30]

[DAY 31]

[DAY 32]

[DAY 35]

Speaking through the Night

Speaking through the Night

Diary of a Lockdown, March–April 2020

Wajdi Mouawad

Translated by Linda Gaboriau

Talonbooks

Talonbooks
9259 Shaughnessy Street, Vancouver, British Columbia, Canada v6p 6r4
talonbooks.com

Talonbooks is located on xʷməθkʷəy̓əm, Sḵwx̱wú7mesh, and səlilwətaɬ Lands.

First printing: 2023

Typeset in Sabon
Printed and bound in Canada on 100% post-consumer recycled paper

Cover image, interior, and cover design by Leslie Smith

Talonbooks acknowledges the financial support of the Canada Council for the Arts, the Government of Canada through the Canada Book Fund, and the Province of British Columbia through the British Columbia Arts Council and the Book Publishing Tax Credit.

Canadä   Canada Council Conseil des arts
for the Arts du Canada   BRITISH COLUMBIA   BRITISH COLUMBIA ARTS COUNCIL An agency of the Province of British Columbia

This work was originally published in French as *Parole tenue* by Leméac Éditeur, Montréal, Québec, in 2021. We acknowledge the financial support of the Government of Canada through the National Translation Program for Book Publishing, an initiative of the *Roadmap for Canada's Official Languages 2013–2018: Education, Immigration, Communities*, for our translation activities.

Library and Archives Canada Cataloguing in Publication

Title: Speaking through the night : diary of a lockdown, March-April 2020 / Wajdi Mouawad ; translated by Linda Gaboriau.
Other titles: Parole tenue. English
Names: Mouawad, Wajdi, author. | Gaboriau, Linda, translator.
Identifiers: Canadiana 20230495702 | ISBN 9781772015393 (softcover)
Subjects: LCSH: Mouawad, Wajdi—Diaries. | LCSH: Dramatists, French-Canadian—Québec (Province)—
    Diaries. | LCSH: COVID-19 Pandemic, 2020-—France—Nogent-sur-Marne—
Personal narratives. | LCGFT:
    Diaries. | LCGFT: Personal narratives.
Classification: LCC PS8576.086 Z46 2023 | DDC C848/.54—dc23

MARCH 2020

MONDAY, MARCH 16, DAY 0

After washing them twice an hour and for thirty seconds every time, my hands have never been so clean as in these days of solitude; yet, despite the cleanliness of my hands, I must be guilty of something. Lady Macbeth without realizing it? What is this stain that remains no matter how hard I scrub? What crime did I commit? Which king's throat did I slit? Unless, in keeping with my era, I am simply one of thousands of Pontius Pilates, another character blinded by the cleanliness of his ten fingers, who wonders what all this has to do with him. If that's the case, who, as I wash my hands, might be sentenced to death today? Which Christ am I sending to crucifixion? What is sublime and dying? What is leaving? Which forest spirit is deserting the world? What must I start grieving? Carefreeness? Two weeks ago, I can't say that I felt carefree: climate change, wildfires, violence towards women, neo-liberalism ... If that is the world this lockdown is forcing me to leave, why hope the lockdown will end as soon as possible? To re-enter which world? Between a world that crushes me and the world that paralyzes me today, how not to feel bewildered? Unable to answer this question, what can I make of this lockdown?

I open my eyes this morning after a night spent wandering in the Bois de Vincennes. What is happening to us? On this first day of confinement, impossible to take stock of the situation, it would be like writing against my nature. I don't know. I don't know what I feel. I have lost the measure of things. I don't know if my lucidity is a form of panic. I go to bed at night thinking that, without realizing it, I might not live to see next summer. Many of us won't. Huge collective grief. I can't be reassured by the increasingly tenuous idea that it will only strike the elderly. And even if that were true, how can the death of others be reassuring? And furthermore, how can we live in a world without the elderly should they all be destined to disappear? No civil war can prevent a pandemic, tragedies come as they please, gods do not exist, there is no logic other than nature and its disruption. Confused thoughts, mixed feelings, multiple sensations, like the pieces of a puzzle with no clear image, just that of dense fog where nothing really fits together: fear, sadness, worry, and memories ... yes ... memories ... like those of the men and women who, like me as a child, experienced a civil war, an epidemic, or a catastrophic event, Fukushima, the earthquake in Haiti, etc. All that contributes to the fog and for reasons that go back to my childhood, I am incapable of hearing the sentence, "In two weeks this will be over, in two months this will be over." That is the sentence I heard as a child about the war in Lebanon. "This will be settled in two months and we will be able to go home. In two months. In six months." It lasted for nineteen years, four hundred thousand deaths later, countless destruction and exiles. So I prefer to hope for the summer rather than count on it. When I told my six-year-old son that his school would be closed because of an epidemic and for an indefinite period, I saw his face light up with the same smile I had on mine when, as a child, I could hear bombs falling. No school. A catastrophe for adults, joy for a child. A young girl my age, with whom I was secretly in love, lived in the building across the street. Enrolled in a different school, she was only accessible to me during air strikes, since we shared the same shelter whenever the bombs started to rain down. Imagine my joy in the chaos of war when our neighbour-hood was targeted. We could be together, in close quarters, we played together, slept together, all the children snuggling close. The joy of the bombardments for the child in 1976, the joy of the epidemic for the child of 2020, the same joy although the causes were different.

It is eight in the evening. I close my eyes and picture the

two halls at Théâtre La Colline, with their respective sets, there on the stage, *Anne-Marie la Beauté* by Yasmina Reza in the small space, *Les innocents, moi et l'inconnue au bord de la route départementale* by Peter Handke in the main space.

I close my eyes and I can hear the silence in the theatre. I close my eyes and visualize the spaces. First the small space, then the big. Having often sat there, I'm very familiar with their silence and the vibration of their emptiness. Then, in my mind, I sit in each seat and I can see the characters, idle, awaiting their incarnation. Poetry has fallen silent. Imagining the hallways in the theatre, I walk down them in my mind, I go from floor to floor, I enter every office, I see the members of the team and I can hear, from afar, from my home, the silence of La Colline and the absence. All of a sudden, a disinherited space. Everyone is cloistered, though devoid of any talent for prayer, and the present shrinks in a duet of syllables: lock-down. Now how can I prevent terror from invading my mind? How to prevent the brutality of thoughts from overwhelming me? How to prevent this from numbing me, crushing me?

So on this first day of confinement, an act of prevention: commit to the practice of writing words to be spoken. Using the networks, one confined human speaking to other confined humans. Once a day, words like windows to break through the brutality of this horizon that is burying us. Writing can also be that: kneading the dough of time. Taking the seconds, the minutes, rolling and folding them to layer time, turning them into other seconds and minutes which, read or heard, will arouse imaginary spaces, for the person writing, for the person listening. Defeat confinement with what makes us human. Words shared.

Like Ariadne's thread that allowed Theseus to retrace his steps. Speaking, words, the human voice, from one to another, like the presence of life in the dark that reassures and offers a fragile sense of peace. Daily texts, a diary kept, like pebbles scattered in a dark night, pebbles on the prisoner's window pane, ricocheting on the surface of a lake and defying drowning, like distant fires sending a signal, speaking of a presence, proof of a presence. Whatever the means. From window to window: open a window and read a poem out loud to the neighbour across the way. Whatever. Offer proof of presence, presence shared in the time of confinement. We are not alone, we continue to be together, in our quest for meaning, though meaning is being brutally, violently tested. I give myself an order: don't forget, a very long time ago, imprisoned with his sailors in the Cyclops's cave, Ulysses, trapped, afraid that he was doomed, managed to overcome the monster thanks to wine, thanks to the *savoir-faire* of his culture. Intoxication vs. death. Today, in this first day of our confinement, aware of the endurance that will be required, dive into writing because it is the only thing that intoxicates me, the only thing I know how to do, that I can do more or less well, the only thing that allows me, even if it remains laughable, to also throw my powers into the battle.

Self-examination as a way of staying in touch with what I love. A mysterious form of connection to the world. To ask myself questions, differently. Like this: when the plague descended upon Thebes, Oedipus sent a messenger to ask the god Apollo to name the reason for this affliction and what could be done to save the city. Oedipus did not yet know that he was both the cause and the remedy of this evil. The plague only struck Thebes. It was limited to Thebes and the troubles of Thebans. What would Apollo answer today if we sent a messenger to his temple, asking for the reason of our affliction? What message would he send, knowing that this calamity is affecting the entire world, north as well as south, east, and west? What would the god of archery reply? What curse? What unsolved hidden crime needs to be elucidated? What responsibility would he ask us to clarify? Would the resolution of the virus reside in the solution that would enable us to imagine a new, better-adjusted approach to living together? Would Apollo say something as inaudible to our ears as: "Restore to the living the portion of life you have stolen from them"?

I took a walk in the silence of night in the Bois de Vincennes. It was still possible. I took advantage of the night, its kindness and the dark shadows of the tall trees. I could hear the rustling and creaking of an invisible world. The silence of the night was marvellous. My irrational fear that I might find myself facing a wild animal, wolf, fox, bear, or sabre-toothed tiger, enchanted me. I am in those woods again because writing brings me back there. During my walk, I thought about my friends, the people I love, and bit by bit my thoughts strayed and suddenly the stories I carry in me which might one day become plays began to walk at my side. Then, a metre away, in the circle of light shed by a lamppost, I noticed the carcass of a turtle. A huge surprise. I bent over. What was it doing here? What brought it to the middle of the woods? It undoubtedly died days, possibly weeks, ago. I dug a hole and buried it. The smell of rain under the earth, the earth under my fingernails, the crunching of the pebbles I disturbed, and the roots of weeds tangled between my fingers. What could anyone who saw me imagine that I was doing? I buried a turtle. A gesture as unexpected as a poem. I stood there in the splendour of the Bois de Vincennes until the dawn of the first day of lockdown.

Walking in the woods for five hours, my mind was in touch with what it loved. The stories that inhabit it, thoughts of my friends, childhood, the forest, the joy of walking in the night. Full, whole, my mind left no room for anything that could rob an ounce of happiness. It became a shield in the face of the toxic fears of a sickness whose only benefit is to make me understand and be aware that I myself am the refuge of my freedom. How to ensure that the time of confinement be a time of living? A time made of something other than waiting for it to end? Perhaps by delving deep into this confinement with writing as the thread that connects me to the world I love.

TUESDAY, MARCH 17, DAY 1

The second day of confinement. Try to concentrate on a simple exercise: the obstinate observation of life being lived according to rules other than those of human beings, life where confinement is not experienced in the same way. For example, take the Japanese maple visible from my window, whose branches are filling with buds. It has been confined to our yard for some twenty years or more, since the previous owners, from whom I purchased the house, planted it. They were a couple, both teachers, who moved to Nogent-sur-Marne towards the middle of the sixties. That was a time when people were slowly turning their backs on the traumatism of the war, rebuilding in the belief of never again, looking cautiously, but with joy, to the future. Those two teachers, who lived in this house where I live now, were witnesses to great transformations. They saw the RER train line, which I take every day, arrive, they undoubtedly appreciated it, they probably went to observe the major road works for the construction of the A4 highway that would soon link them to Paris in less than fifteen minutes and eliminate the passage of trailer trucks on the roads of their town; long before the installation of the electronic network, they saw towns and cities connected via the network of highways and railroads, joining the ripples that separated them, the ripples we call the suburbs. They saw small businesses close to make way for bigger ones, and they witnessed the destruction of old working-class houses to make way for concrete. Nogent-sur-Marne was still almost the countryside. I think about that countryside so distant today when I look out my window and see the houses of my neighbours, confined to their homes like me. We don't talk to each other, rarely say so much as hello. Nogent is a pretty, cautious town. Today there are still a few open-air cafés but they are more folkloric than real, and the town is no longer home to the working class. Yet despite the suspicious tendencies I sense beneath the surface, I like this town because I recognize the wave of immigration I knew when, fleeing the war in Lebanon, my family briefly took refuge in Paris. That was in 1978 and in those days, some Lebanese had the means to live in the 16th and 7th arrondissements, and while others, despite their dreams, could only afford to live in the 15th arrondissement. At the time, the 15th was home to the wave of petit-bourgeois Lebanese immigrants who had achieved some lower-middle-class status and were determined to forget the poverty of their working-class origins. My family, despite their aspirations, could not afford the fancier neighbourhoods. So during my five years in Paris, the worst years of the war in Lebanon, I grew up in the neighbourhoods around boulevard de Grenelle where my neighbours were Lebanese, Romanian, Yugoslavian, or Czech immigrants. Today Nogent-sur-Marne has become the best option for a social class of immigrants – Polish, Lebanese, Romanian – who can't afford to live in the 15th, which has become what the 16th represented to my parents more than forty years ago: the Holy Grail of high society. That is what I find so touching about Nogent. I recognize myself. Myself as a child. It is, moreover, a pleasant town. I sense that it will be easy to be confined here because it has become a place made for confinement. And it has its share of mysteries. There is the Maison nationale des artistes. This retirement home for artists has a magnificent wooded park. I often go walking there at night. There are many community services available in Nogent. We live between the Marne River and the Pavillon Baltard, and the Bois de Vincennes is within walking distance for those who like to walk. Something, however, is off in this town, something that has no name, that seems to think only about itself. Certain signs are blatant. The most dramatically eloquent in my opinion is that Nogent-sur-Marne doesn't have a bookstore. To find a book in Nogent, you have to visit the shop that serves as a stationery store, a newsstand, and a bookstore. They carry the books of the year and those that have won literary prizes, but the choice remains rudimentary. You come out of the shop without having met anyone with whom you could chat about an author. Yet, in the 1980s in Nogent-sur-Marne, there was a mythical bookstore, the Librarie Berthet. André Berthet, who had been a butcher before turning to books, is a towering figure in the history of the book trade in France. He trained many young people who have become influential booksellers today in Paris, Nantes, Bordeaux, and elsewhere, and in whom he inculcated an approach to books and to readers that is more combative than commercial. André Berthet had one principle: anyone who enters his bookstore absolutely must leave with a book! Anyone who enters the store with the intention of buying a particular book absolutely must leave with two books! There is a veritable mythology about this unusual man. The story goes that, should someone ask for a book not available on his shelves, he would go so far as to ask the customer to watch over the shop while he jumped into his car and promptly went to procure the book from the publisher. When Antoine Gallimard came to visit him and asked how he managed to sell so many books in the luxury Bibliothèque de la Pléiade edition, apparently André Berthet didn't bat an eyelash and replied, "You know, Monsieur Gallimard, when you've managed to sell boudin sausage, you can sell Pléiades books." His bookstore closed in 2007. Since then, nothing. It is sad enough to live in a town with no bookstores, but this sadness is accentuated every time I pass by the storefronts that once were home to Monsieur Berthet's bookstore, the store I never knew, that I would have loved to know, and every time I am dismayed to see that part of the space is now occupied by a medical-testing laboratory and the other part by a real estate agency. So here I am looking out my window on this second day of confinement. What book would Monsieur Berthet have recommended to me if I had paid him a clandestine visit? The Japanese maple in my yard is so beautiful. It was there in my yard when Monsieur Berthet opened his store and there when it closed, it was there every day Monsieur Berthet sold a book, it was there for every book sold, for every book read. It was always there, although confined to the yard, it was there. What secret, what advice, what magic words would the trees murmur to us today if we could hear them? They, even more than prisoners, know what it means to be confined. The Japanese maple raises its branches to the light. This week it will undoubtedly display the tender green of its leaves. Since I am here every day, every morning brings a chance to observe its colours and the slightest change in its colours. And more than that, a chance to see how day after day the sunlight bathes its leaves, and see how differently it bathes the leaves from one day to the next, and in this way learn more about the orbit of the planets. That will undoubtedly do me more good than remaining glued to the news that only manages to shrink my thoughts. The maple is already covered in buds. And the tulips, at its feet, are disrobing and raising their joyful heads. The grass in the yard is finally breathing again. Yet all of that is confined. The tree in the yard is confined, the tulips confined in their tub. But that is their nature. Their way of being. In dialogue with light, with water. Living rooted, knowing nothing of movement, except that of the wind in their branches, their petals. The trees, the plants are there, for the birds. So if I am a tree, what birds would there be for me? Perhaps my thoughts, my dreams, are my birds. Perhaps that is why we sometimes say that someone was "visited by an idea." To be visited by an idea, the way a tree is visited by a bird. An idea, a thought, an image, and what if the power of the human mind consisted of its capacity to make an idea appear, as if a tree, through a mere act of will, could make birds appear? Clearly those birds would be magnificent, magic birds, existential birds with the gift of speech. So if I am the magic tree that gives birth to birds, I would like to give birth to the ideas that lift me towards life. I'm looking at the small yard around the house. The colours are so vivid! Springtime! Springtime!! The birds come and go, the cat doesn't change his habits. From the window, I can see him, I can watch the ritual gathering of all the little felines in the back lane. There are ants in the house. There are ants outdoors. They come and go. Today there was even a butterfly, the first of the year. It entered the room and flitted around before landing on the table where I write. On this second day of confinement, I observe the living things that are not human and I can see how they, within their reality, are indifferent to our experience and, for them, life goes on. I never bother the spiders that spin their webs on the wall of my study. I leave them alone, and in a certain way we are living together, I live in their company. For the most part, they are rather large European garden spiders. Very likeable, if I may say so. Neither dangerous nor aggressive, they rid my house of aphids and mosquitoes. Incredible weavers. I believe, from what I've been able to observe, their lifespan is fourteen days. I often let their carcasses dry on the wood floor before placing them in a matchbox. When the box is full of dead spiders from the room where I write, I bury it at the foot of the Japanese maple. The sun is setting. One after the other, the neighbours' children, then mine, go out to play in the back lane. Something is beyond our grasp. Something is happening inside us, through us, something that frightens us is in the process of transforming us. From time to time I tell myself, quietly, almost inaudibly, then I tell others, yes, sometimes I tell myself that there are disasters thanks to which, horribly, we manage to experience unsuspected joys. I watch my children playing. These children, I must say it because everything in our situation today reminds me of this, these children exist because the war in Lebanon existed, because the war in Lebanon disrupted the lives of so many Lebanese families. Including my parents. But if the war in Lebanon hadn't existed, I wouldn't have left my country, the life I would have lived would have been different, happy, even marvellous, perhaps, but I can say in all certainty that the two children playing there, in the lane, the children I love and who some twenty times a day call me Papa, those two children wouldn't have existed. This thought brings tears to my eyes and, strangely, gives me the strength to feel hope in the face of the disaster that has currently struck our lives.

WEDNESDAY, MARCH 18, DAY 2

The minute I woke up, I realized the day was going to be brutal. One of those famous days where you say to yourself, this is just one of those days. It was awaiting me at dawn, staring me in the face, saying, "Here I am, I'm just one of those days and I'll hound you until night comes to blot me out." I have to admit that since my return from Strasbourg where I was supposed to perform in a show that was cancelled on last Friday the thirteenth when gatherings of more than one hundred people were forbidden, since that day, I have been counting the days.

I haven't been counting the days, looking forward, like the prisoner anticipating the end of his sentence – how could we, confined to our homes by the lockdown, possibly know when our sentence will end? – but I have been counting backwards, because that day of my return from Strasbourg was the last moment I spent in the presence of a crowd, in the street, at the train station, in the Métro, on my way home. An interminable odyssey of several hours. I am counting the days, anxiously waiting, like so many others, to reach day fourteen, the new Everest, to know whether I have been incubated, or not. This word, *incubated*, which I use intentionally because I love its grim evocation and the clinically repulsive reactions it triggers in me, takes me back to the extraordinary sequence in the first *Alien* movie when one of the crew members has his face attacked by the creature that will inseminate him with the Alien who will incubate in him, procreate through him. In short, what inseminates us intends to kill us. The way to resist this enemy, for us common mortals, is not to engage in a hand-to-hand combat, for the enemy is bound to win, but rather to use the strategy of the void. Crush the Alien through the void. A physical void and a spiritual overflow. But am I empty? This question triggers, after the Ridley Scott film, the image of Linda Blair's face in *The Exorcist*. She is also haunted, confined from within her body, by the invisible. But today, for us, there is no courageous priest who will trace the Trinity on our faces to extract the evil. No. To know whether we are touched by this evil, we are sentenced to count to fourteen. And I am counting to fourteen. In the face of this exhausting hypochondria, against which I sometimes fail to raise the shield of rational thought, I'm stunned to realize that I can no longer remember what comes after fourteen. I simply know that, at home with my family, if I reach fourteen with none of the symptoms related to this incubation, I'll feel, more or less, at least temporarily, reassured.

I knew in advance that the day was going to be brutal and that its mood would be dictated by the creed of anxiety. And this anxiety is so powerful that it makes me understand, acutely, the anxiety I sensed in my mother as she paced back and forth in the bomb shelters after every explosion, profusely cursing "them all" who were doing this to us. Today I remember my mother's anxiety and I finally understand, as I feel it myself, that her anxiety was for us and not for herself. A mother's anxiety is as innate as one's mother tongue. Confined in the shelters, we children had no idea what our parents were going through. Or perhaps we had an idea but our confidence in them was greater than anything we could imagine, as long as they were there, as long as they were there so anxious, this meant that they were looking after us and we were protected. That is what I should remember. The anxiety I feel today, in its restraint, in what escapes me, in some ways protects and proves to the children that I am there for them, it reassures them more than it worries them because if they felt no anxiety on my part, their intelligence, which alerts them to the danger, might make them feel that the adult who is at their sides, accompanying them, has no sense of the danger. In the shelter, it was my mother's anxiety that provided the space for us to play. And our favourite game was to guess the type of cannons and the calibre of the bombs falling around us. That required great subtlety. A barely perceptible boom might mean either that the bomb had struck far away, or, on the contrary, that it was the detonation of a cannon that had just fired a bomb heading in our direction. Distinguishing one boom from another was extremely difficult. All ears, we tried to guess and chalk up points. Meanwhile my mother counted the seconds, constantly expecting to see the shelter ripped open by an explosion which, like a bullish monster, would shred us to pieces. Four decades later, I am counting the days, expecting to feel, from one minute to the next, the first symptoms: fever, cough, suffocation. Yes, this is an awful day. As soon as I opened my eyes, I knew I'd be struggling with sadness and fear. Watching *Sing* with my children, in the hope that the joy of the music and the amusing situations would lift our spirits, I was suddenly overcome, towards the end of the film, in the scene where Buster Moon gives his show, by an irrepressible sob, as if the immense joy communicated by the film had become, in a single second, without warning, nostalgia for former times. And I understood that what's happening today, what I find so upsetting, is not the memory of the war in Lebanon, nor is it an intellectualized understanding of the historic situation we find ourselves in, but rather the realization that we are sinking, we are entering a long bout. That we need to say goodbye to many things. That we are about to understand that this is not a nightmare, we are wide awake, and we are about to grasp the magnitude of the challenge ahead. That we are about to understand, about to feel, if we take the time, what Ulysses felt when he realized that he was a prisoner on Calypso's island. He had survived so many trials, defeated the Cyclops, escaped from the sirens and other dangers, lost all his companions before landing there, on Calypso's fabulous island, where, having fallen in love with him, the nymph refuses to let him leave. Ulysses could easily wonder why the gods continued to persecute him. Hadn't he known enough grief? Hadn't he lost everything? Hadn't he spent ten years fighting the war of Troy and now been confined for another seven years on Calypso's island? Why must he face tribulation after tribulation? This makes me think about the humans who having been through the Great War went through the Second World War. Violence clearly doesn't neutralize violence. There is no quota of unhappiness. There is no quota, no one on high to say, "Fine. That's enough. Enough for that man, for that era, for that generation, the quota has been reached." No. Far from Ithaca, convinced he would never see his home again, Ulysses longed for Ithaca. How happy he would be if he could return home and see his house. For centuries the poets have sung and we have repeated:

Happy the one who, like Ulysses,
has taken a marvellous journey,
or like him who won the golden fleece,
and then comes home, full of wisdom and knowledge,
to live among his family the rest of his days!

Alas, when will I see the smoke from the chimneys
of my little village, and what time of year
will I sit within the garden walls of my humble house,
which to me is a province and much more?

But now the world is upside down: today we are confined to our homes. I am in my house. And I will have to remain here. In my home. Precisely. And where is the happiness in that? Yet, "Happy like Ulysses." Why do we feel that this poem is upside down today? Unless we are the ones who are seeing the world wrong? Perhaps we have been walking upside down for years, not realizing that what seems to be upright is upside down like this poem.

On this third day of confinement at home, in our respective Ithacas, our houses, many surrounded by those closest and dearest, their Penelope, their Telemachus, we are filled with longing, like Ulysses. But what are we longing for, since we are at home? Has Calypso's island become home, and home become Calypso's island? Are we waiting for Athena to set us free? From what? For what? From the course of life.

Unless our situation is less like that of Ulysses, more like that of another famous prisoner who, during the same era, is sentenced to confinement for a long time. "In the six-hundredth year of Noah's life, in the second month, the seventeenth day of the month, that very day, the same day were all the fountains of the great deep broken up, and the windows of heaven were opened. And the rain was upon the earth forty days and forty nights ... And the Lord shut him in." The mythical lockdown imposed on Noah and his sons and all the creatures of the earth, all together on the ark. Perhaps we are the descendants of Noah and, from generation to generation, we still await the end of the flood, but since that story is no longer told nor transmitted to us, we have forgotten. The dove never returned with the olive branch and that was also forgotten. Perhaps, in fact, the dove returned more than once to show us the path, but no longer knowing what she represented, having forgotten what she symbolized, even forgetting why she returned, we couldn't understand what she came to teach us. The animals who were with us on the ark, who were there to save all the species, came to represent our survival. We have slaughtered them, devoured them. More than once we have slaughtered each other and now at the end of this long march, in a time of peace and sunshine, in the springtime – springtime! – our ark is ship-wrecked on an invisible coast. I lie here while everyone is asleep. This long day is coming to an end with the image of Noah's ark. Like a gift. An image that calms me because it helps me understand what is happening to us. Something about this lockdown reminds me of Noah's plight. Or rather his confinement helps me reflect. That's how panic is. We no longer know how to reflect. I open the Bible, I reread the chapter. Now I understand the passage differently. I receive it differently. Our situation sheds new light on the text. It is no longer a myth. It speaks to me directly. It even reassures me. Our ark is immense, it is composed of all the languages on Earth, composed of our entire humanity. What I am feeling, what I am experiencing is being felt, experienced by a great number of human beings around the world at the moment when I am writing these lines. The day the floods recede, when the doors of the ark open and we step onto land again, what new world will we need to build? Our origins will be separate from our identities. And to those who will be born later, we will say that we are those born before the lockdown, but our identity, our new identity, was forged by it, thanks to it. Greater than the feat of surviving this trial, the trial of rising to the lessons we have learned will undoubtedly be the challenge of our era. And we should undoubtedly begin to think about this now. In dramaturgical terms, this could be called plotting a story of victory.

THURSDAY, MARCH 19, DAY 3

I hope, as I keep this diary come what may, inspired or not, whether writing comes easily or not, I hope I can stay on the byways, I hope to follow the paths that lead away from the highway, to find clearings, even if it means losing my way in the woods, rather than adhering to the reality of "current events." My reasons for avoiding that are many, but one reason is that I hope, in writing, that I will never offend, despite myself, the people who are under the full fire of the plague every day. That's why I will avoid descriptions of the reality and try, with every entry, to crack open this reality to reveal a perspective that will help me move away from the glass I keep hitting, like the fly that persists, incapable of understanding this invisible barrier that prevents it from flying away. Unable to see that the window is ajar, right there to the side, the fly keeps hitting the invisible wall of glass, again and again. Obstinately it persists, flies in circles before returning to strike the obstacle it cannot grasp. But I mustn't judge the fly that persists, how often have I persisted, repeatedly hitting what I refused to admit? So I will write to avoid the trap of dwelling on the latest news, to avoid the temptation of the media for a few hours. Writing, painting, playing, loving, cooking, clowning around, showing off, inventing silly wordplay, napping, never going back to that glass wall, back rather to my pen, and writing again, because from writing, the very act of writing, images emerge that would not emerge otherwise. And these images, these ideas, these associations between one thing and another, create a perspective, a depth, that allows me to see beyond the tip of my nose. It often doesn't take much. It's a question of finding the path, the angle that reveals the vanishing point, to escape, vanish, a question of finding an unexpected image, an image with no apparent logic, out of nowhere, escaping causality (if I'm thinking about this, it's because I was thinking about this) and capturing my thought. For example. Now. Close my eyes and think about the Chauvet Cave. The Chauvet Cave. The lions. The bison. The stencilled hands on the walls. That was thirty-five thousand years ago. The Chauvet Cave is still there. While we are living through what we are living through. The Chauvet Cave. The lions. The paintings of lions are there. At this very moment, they are there. The great mystery of those lions, and the mystery of the person who painted them thirty-five thousand years ago. They are there. No matter what happens, they will be there. That's so encouraging! The eternal night of those paintings. Think, concentrate, close your eyes and imagine approaching the walls. Standing just behind the painter. That was long before the great massacres, before the wars, the exiles, before the great fear. Now, smell the odour of the stone, go closer, smell the wall, smell the paint. Listen. Hear the scratching on the wall of the charcoal the painter is holding. Now think of the caves not yet discovered, still secret, that will be discovered in one hundred or two hundred years. They are already there. No one who has been a witness of our times will be on this earth to bear witness. There will be images, stories, of us. A memory. Think about the tombs of kings that are still to be found, think that now, right now, while I am writing these lines, then recording what I have written, in this very moment, twenty thousand leagues under the sea, lie Spanish galleons. There, in the depths, there are fish not yet named. There is still much to be discovered on earth. Think about all that, and then the fly, suddenly noticing the window is ajar, makes an enormous effort to put an end to its obsessive patterns and finally finds the opening to escape.

Musing like this, writing what I find at hand, I think about the Hermitage Museum. I close my eyes and start exploring its corridors in a single-shot sequence, like Sokurov's film

Russian Ark, shot in one unedited sequence which, in cinema, could be called a confinement shot since once the shot is undertaken, once the camera begins shooting, there is no question of stopping until the action is over, and in this regard, Sokurov's *Russian Ark*, a single-shot sequence of ninety-six minutes, goes beyond and captures confinement with an elegance rarely achieved. So I strike out down the corridors of the Hermitage Museum in my thoughts, and in my thoughts I pay no attention to the Rubenses or the Vermeers, I move ahead blindly until I reach hall 254 of the museum. This hall is reserved for Rembrandt. I stop. Two huge paintings hang facing each other. *The Return of the Prodigal Son* on one side and *The Sacrifice of Isaac* on the other. They face each other. The two paintings look at each other. For the visitor, looking at one means turning one's back to the other. Two paintings by Rembrandt, two paintings depicting a father and son. In *The Sacrifice of Isaac,* there is the innocent son, Isaac, and his father about to sacrifice him under God's command. *The Return of the Prodigal Son,* on the other hand, on the other side of the hall, depicts a son guilty of having squandered his inheritance welcomed lovingly by his father. On one side, divine law overrides a father's love, on the other side, a father's love overrides human law. Beyond the power of the paintings, this presentation places the visitor physically between two radically different positions. "Where do you stand?" the two paintings seem to ask the visitor. The visitor is confronted with these conflicting notions: law or love, justice or morality. In my little house in Nogent, I am thinking of the two paintings still hanging, as I write, in the Hermitage Museum, facing each other, and a certain intuition tells me that one of them regards our current situation. So, on this fourth day of lockdown, I took the time to consider the question; studying both paintings in a book on Rembrandt in my library, I came to the conclusion that our situation is more related to the painting depicting the law than the painting depicting love, more akin to the sacrifice of Isaac than to the welcome of the prodigal son. I place the book on the table. I look at the painting and I describe it. It's nighttime, or dusk. Isaac lies on the arid mountain ground, his hands tied behind his back, bare-chested. His skin, as pale as the moon, the brightness of his throat, his neck bent back under the weight of his father's hand that covers, crushes his face, perhaps so it won't be visible when he kills him, reveals the youth and the innocence of the child. The most extraordinary detail is that Isaac doesn't seem to be struggling, the grandeur of the son, grandeur of youth, grandeur of Isaac, as if he totally accepted his father's will. Above him Abraham, whose face is strangely impassive, is following divine orders, showing no hesitation, no fear, except perhaps in his gesture to hide his son's face. Above Abraham, in the upper left-hand corner of the painting, emerging from the night, an angel holds back the father's hand, the hand holding the knife, as if, at the last instant, the instant when the blade is about to slit the child's throat, something sublime, something immense, something unexpected, something extraordinary intervenes to prevent the father's fatal gesture towards his son.

I look at this painting and I'm flabbergasted, stupefied! Something has fallen into place, like the coincidence between two pieces of a puzzle that have absolutely nothing to do with each other. I look at the angel in the painting and I think about the messages I received today from some of my friends. Is it true or not? I don't know, but apparently fish have reappeared in the lagoon in Venice, they said that even dolphins have been spotted. They say that now stars are visible in the night sky over Paris. In the newspaper, one meteorological map illustrates the density of pollution over China before the pandemic and another shows that of today. Heaviness gives way to lightness. They also say that the consumption of electricity has diminished drastically. They say that human beings are waking up to something. They say that animals are returning. That the sky is breathing. That machines are slowing down. They say that something is stirring! I stare at the painting, the angel, Abraham, Isaac, the knife in the instant before the sacrifice. Could it be that humanity was Abraham, obeying this law that has become divine over time, thanks to this often-monstrous period of peace, the law of exploitation and brutality and the use we make of this world, to paraphrase the marvellous title that sounds like a prophesy today? Could humanity have been Abraham obeying this law? And might we be Abraham about to slit the throat of everything he loved the most? Life itself, youthful life, the life of children, of future generations? And what if, barrelling ahead in this obedience to a law become divine, we, Abraham, our humanity, were unable to stop, didn't know how to stop, how to arrest the fatal gesture, the bloodletting, and the appearance of an angel were the only solution? What could that angel possibly be? What can that angel be? Could the virus be an angel holding back our hand about to murder everything dear to us? Could this exterminating angel be trying to tell us something immense? I stare at the Rembrandt painting, I see the hand of the angel gripping Abraham's hand. In the Scriptures, it is said that after that night, a new alliance was established between Abraham and his God. What alliance might we forge among ourselves? What are the words to name it, and who can write it? For ages humans have been brought together by language. What then are the new words? How can we give new meaning to the words of the tribe?

Like the tides, sensitive to the phases of the moon, our nocturnal dreams are sensitive to the shocks and catastrophes that befall us. Our dreams are their echo more real than the primal scream. Like messages we send ourselves from the strata where our terrors live, night after night, our dreams conjure indecipherable visions. As if we had a vital need to remain incomprehensible, indecipherable to ourselves. Yet, often through quotidian situations, every dream makes us feel vivid sensations and emotions that become real experiences in their own right. Dreaming in our sleep, we are both captive and free inside our image-making machine. What could be more otherworldly than a dream, yet what could be more convincing? It was last night. I am at home, I know I'm housebound with my family, and suddenly my house seems empty. Where are the children? I can't manage to call out. Something irreversible seems to have happened. I am overcome by terror. I am stumbling. In the little hallway between the kitchen and my daughter's bedroom, I discover a spiral staircase I had never noticed before. I'm ashamed. How could I have missed such a thing? I want to climb it when, in a flash, I remember that this staircase leads to the beach, and it seems perfectly normal that the Parisian rooftops overlook the sea. I had completely forgotten that. I listen, I can hear the sea, I can even smell the salt in the air, and now I can hear the children laughing. They're there. They're there! A great wave of relief reassures me, sets me free. Like a branch buried under the weight of snow freed by the spring thaw, all of a sudden a burst of weightlessness makes my heart leap. I hear my partner call out casually, "Be careful, the sun is shining but the air is cool!" and never has a sentence seemed so cheery! I go up the steps as quickly as possible, I go up the steps and I'm hit by a thought I keep repeating to myself, incredulous: "It's over! It's over! We can go out!" and as I turn around the axis of spiral staircase leading to the roof, racing to join them, racing to see the sea, I take a step and I wake up before getting outside. I lay in my bed frozen, hardly breathing, hoping to conserve this feeling of freedom and happiness. And gradually, I came to, I reintegrated real time, so to speak. My first thought was about people, my neighbours, others, the Parisians, the French, the Italians, people everywhere, and I wondered whether other people, in lockdown somewhere, had also had a dream related in some way to what we are experiencing. Statistically it is very likely. It appeared self-evident to me, perfectly normal. Our nocturnal dreams have begun to change. And they will undoubtedly change even more. Today one billion people are housebound. A billion dreams dreamed every night, each vibrating, increasingly, to the measure of this crisis making it possible that, from one night to the next, as the lockdown continues, every dream of every human will have something in common with the dreams of the nine hundred ninety-nine million nine hundred ninety-nine thousand other human beings. It's probable, conceivable. Never has a single trauma, affecting so many people, sentenced everyone to isolate themselves in such a common, ordinary, and intimate place: their home. With all the inequalities that exist between the houses, with all the difficulties that exist for some and not for others, we are all, nevertheless, cloistered in our designated private spaces, at home, in a closed space we cannot leave, our houses. Our homes. We are at home. Every one of us. At home. Nothing is smaller than the surface of a face, and yet nothing is more unlimited than the diversity of faces. That can be said of homes as well. Nothing is more cloistered and nothing more diverse. Most of our homes include a kitchen, a bed, walls, a window, a door to enter and exit. They don't have the same floor plan, but to a great extent, the same essential functions are served. Like a face: eyes, cheeks, mouth, nose, ears, forehead for everyone, but rarely do we encounter two identical examples despite the limited space on which this facial geography is arranged. And this link, between face and house, contributes more than we think to the sense of confinement. Faces of flesh confined in their faces of stone. Given this mystery, it's possible to imagine that, should our confinement continue much longer, once seven billion humans find themselves barricaded, one night, without knowing it, with some variations, with varying details, one night, seven billion people will have the same dream. And what would this dream be? Humanity, together, having the same dream. It is said that in archaic tribes, the menstrual cycles of all the women became the same, in synchronicity with the phases of the moon. Perhaps, therefore, rebecoming archaic without realizing it, after the confinement is over, all humanity, in synchronicity with the tides, with the flights of birds, will have the same dream. This would be the first time since the most ancient times, since a group of *Homo sapiens* lived together, sharing the same territory, long before the first migrations. As I write this, I see the monolith in *2001: A Space Odyssey* rise before me, I approach it trembling, I touch it with my fingertips, and I grasp more fully the genius of the ellipsis Stanley Kubrick stages in his film, between the flight of the yak thigh bone thrown by early man and the fall of the spaceship thousands of years later. A link, an experience from seventy thousand years ago that could be repeated a second time today. The human tribe in 2020, one night, dreaming the same dream. The odyssey of an osmosis, a tribal solidarity. Why should this perspective seem absurd? Don't people say there are nightmares related to certain corporations? Certain trades? Actors, a corporation I know well, share a terrifying dream most of them admit to having had at least once in their life: they are about to go on stage, in the middle of a performance, having absolutely no idea which show they are performing in, having forgotten to memorize their lines, incapable of remembering a single action! They want to escape but they can't, everyone is counting on them, the scene depends upon them, they have to go on now, they tell themselves they'll have to improvise ... just before they wake up drenched in sweat. In the nightmare of directors, with some variations, the audience gets up and leaves while the actors go on performing the best they can, or in another nightmare the directors stand by as the actors rebel and start to perform something else, another script, in another staging. Every trade, every corporation has common nightmares and dreams related to their work. That's because among the members of every profession there is a solidarity related to the stress and anxiety inherent in that profession. During the civil war, we all ended up having the same nightmares, archetypical situations, houses destroyed, houses on fire, parents disappeared. Didn't the survivors of the concentration camps have the same dreams of escape and freedom? Don't astronauts in the space station, after eight months of confinement in the immensity of the universe, end up sharing equivalent dreams? If the billions of humans isolated today were all actors, sooner or later they would all have the same nightmare, and if they were all firemen, they would undoubtedly share the fundamental nightmare of firemen. So this lockdown is imposing a solidarity, still preliminary, still fragile, among the French under lockdown for the past week, but what about the Chinese, what about the Italians, who have been enduring this for several weeks? What if it were to go on for a year? Would we have a single, same dream? And what would this dream be, beyond the languages and cultures involved? The dream probably doesn't matter, what matters is the possibility that the dream could come true. If we had to choose, personally I would imagine a dream bearing witness to memory. A dream where, miraculously, we could hear the voices of the loved ones who have disappeared in the battle. The dreams in which we meet loved ones who disappeared feel so true. We would all dream, all seven billion humans, each one in the same night at the end of the confinement, that, sleeping in the room where we really sleep, we wake up to drink a glass of water when, suddenly, the ghosts of those we love and who love us are sitting at the foot of our bed, watching us. At first, we would be terrified, but then, peacefully, one of these ghosts, father, mother, son, uncle, grandfather, friend, husband, wife, lover, professor, colleague, would pronounce, ever so gently, a simple word, perhaps simply our name, but in such a manner, so clearly, that suddenly we would feel transported by immense confidence, vivid confidence, a confidence in ourselves so obvious, so full of goodness, free of all pettiness, a confidence that enables us to wake up full of new ardour. Perhaps in that night of a single dream, on the threshold of the end of our confinement, after so many nights, so many days, the dead, with their prophetic gift, will offer to us, the living, an unshakeable confidence in life so we can rise and finally leave our homes.

TUESDAY, MARCH 24, DAY 8

If it took God six days to create the world and the universe, resting on the seventh, today, as I woke up, I thought of Him and a sort of proud joy came over me, prompting me to tell this God who's been bugging us since Creation: **You can stuff your seven days, look at us, we just entered our eighth, try to do better, so there!** It was with that feeling of victory and self-satisfied confidence in the human race that I got up this morning, determined to do something with my two hands, to be useful in the battle that humanity wages in the silence of the heavens. But in no time, the day took an unexpected turn. I spent the morning of this eighth day with my six-year-old son, grappling with the sound he had to master today according to the "homeschooling" plan his teacher sent us and which we are following scrupulously. An activity as necessary and obligatory for him as for me. Except – the sound he was supposed to learn today wasn't the simplest of sounds. On the contrary. It wasn't the **oi** or the **ou**, nor was it the **é** or **on**, but the much sneakier, more perverse, less obvious, almost hypocritical, vague, undecided, uncertain, it was the most painful sound a child in grade one could encounter, I'm talking of course about the **gn**, the unpronounceable, unbearable sound, undoubtedly the worst of all: **gn**. Of all the sounds in the French language, **gn** is the least popular. Just think about it: how many of us find the strength to complete the **gn** sound when we say **montagne** or **ligne** or even more horrendous, **baignoire**? By the time we leave early childhood, we often take many things for granted, and the more we take them for granted, the more careless we become, making room for our natural laziness that results in a flattening, a flabbiness, not only of our body and its verticality, but also of our relationship to language, and therefore to sound, including, among all the sounds, the perverse *gn*, and without realizing it we begin to adopt the wrong pronunciation, and we do so with a shameless confidence that cultivates a peremptory attitude towards the *gn* sound, allowing us to say things like, "*That's the way I am, you know, I've got my principles,* on ne me fera pas faire n'importe quoi, *I am who I am,* point à la line. *Period.*" Or in chatting with a colleague, a subordinate, of course, we will announce, making it clear that he has a long way to go before he attains our relationship to freedom, "*You know, after this rough patch at work, I think I'm going to take a break, yeah, I'm going to take the wife and kids and, I don't know, we'll head for the mountains, right, we'll go skiing,* en montane." Isn't it great to be able to gush and say, "*Ah là là, comme la montane est belle aujourd'hui.*" That's what we say. *La montane. Point à la line.* Of course not everyone practises such a lack of respect for the *gn* sound in *montagne* or *ligne*, some people still care about their diction, but who today is capable of pronouncing the word *magnifique* enunciating the *gn* sound in the middle of the word? Having made that case so clearly, now how do I explain, on this eighth day of the lockdown, to a six-year-old boy, that while the *gn* sound in *champignon* is written *g-n*, that sound in the word *panier* is written *n-i*. How? The boy raised his head and, with good reason, turned to his father with a look of indescribable confusion, as if, in facing the challenge of *gn* he was encountering the incoherence of the adult world, "*But, Papa, if the gn sound in panier is written with n-i, why is the gn in champignon written g-n?*" It was difficult to explain to a child who has an acute sense of injustice why, why the *gn* sound in *panier* doesn't deserve the *gn* in *champignon. Especially,* he said, *since we use baskets,* paniers, *to gather our mushrooms,* champignons. What possible answer! And then try to convince him that the word *magnifique* in which he couldn't hear the *gn* is written with a *g-n*, so why isn't that sound in the word *panier* written with a *g-n* too? And what's more, really, if *panier* can be written simply with an n, why not write *champignon* that way too? And the same for *baignoire* and *gagner*, all these words could be written with just an *n* and simply get rid of this impossible *gn*, my son concludes, "The *gn* is totally useless!" Not quite, I tried to reply to save the dignity of *gn*. *Montagne* and *ligne* need it, I said. *"But, Papa, you said that adults don't bother to pronounce it, and everyone still manages to go hiking on the montane, or go racing to the finish line, what's the point of this useless sound*?!" And while I imagined this homework would be simple, he and I spent the entire morning today on these insoluble questions, grappling with *oignons*, *signes*, *baignoires*, *grognements*, *gagnants*, and *cigognes* and all the other aggravating *gn* words. And the day went by. It's been a week since I left the house. I did what countless other people like me must have done, cleaning radiators with a toothbrush, finally reaching those inaccessible creases. I devoted two days to new apple tart recipes, only to conclude that I don't have the manual skill of a pastry chef, I tried to repair the washing machine and tried to understand why the refrigerator was leaking, only to conclude that, really, I am not gifted manually. Sometimes, around eight in the evening, I'd go to the window and my awkward hands would applaud, and amused, my son would come to applaud with me, only to declare with disconcerting certainty, *"Papa, this is stupid because all the doctors and nurses are taking care of sick people in the hospitals, with a roof over their heads and walls all around them, and machines going beep, beep, beep, so they can't hear us applauding."* "You're right, they can't hear us applauding." *"So why are we applauding?"* "Well, you see, it's like the *gn* in *magnifique*. We can't hear it, but it's there to remind us that *magnifique* comes from *magnus* meaning 'great' in Latin." *"But Papa, we're not Latin. You're an Arab and I'm a Jew."* "Precisely," I said, "that's the definition of *gn*." And it was nighttime. *gn gn gn gn gn gn gn gn.* Useless.

In fact, that's what I am, useless. Exactly that, a useless *gn*. And the last time I was overcome by this paradoxical uselessness was at this little boy's birth. What, indeed, can a man do when the child is busy, with his mother, being born? Nothing! The most a man can do is to be there, without interfering, without getting in the way, without touching a thing, simply be there, present. And to remark afterwards, "That was all I could do, I was there, I was worried, I was involved." Some might say that's not useless. Yes, it's useless, I would say, like the *gn* in *magnifique*. And as *magnifique* as giving birth can be, as *magnifique* as the woman giving birth, as the child being born can be, the man is the *gn*, the sound not heard in the *magnifique* event taking place. A man is useless at the moment of birth. And I find it annoying to pretend otherwise, since all the arguments to the contrary remain mere figures of speech. And now, in this situation, the same sensation. In this enormous reality born of the tragedy we are all experiencing, in these our times which have finally reached the ravine that has been looming ahead, feared but impossible to define, the men and women who are attending the birth, who are in the heat of the battle of this backward birth that consists of saving lives, for whom we must make room, are, first of all, those front line health-care workers, then the men and women who ensure the distribution of essential products to the population, from the farmer to the local grocer, then the men and women who preside over public services and have the responsibility of governing us. And the journalists who keep us informed and all the teams who maintain the networks that deliver electricity, the internet, gas, and hot water, including the garbage collectors. They are the only ones who can be considered useful today. But the rest of us are like fathers waiting for the child's birth. How to deal with this sense of total uselessness when we suspect that this is just the beginning? On this cool, sunny afternoon, standing at the window, staring at the blue sky, I caught myself repeating *gn gn gn gn gn*, *magnifique*, *baignoire*, *baignoire*.

Then I remembered my own French lessons when I arrived in Paris in 1978 at the age of ten and had to learn this sophisticated language I barely spoke. Why was the *f* sound sometimes written with a *p* and an *h*? "Don't try to understand, just accept it," I was told, and I accepted, learning without understanding, with no one to tell me that the *ph* was the Indo-European phoneme associated with light, hence *phoenix*, *physical*, *photography*, and that the French language had conserved it to remember the languages from which it had evolved. And there was the conjugation of the verb *aller*, "to go," always making the same mistakes, *je alle* ..., and having my fingers rapped before writing out ten times, *je vais, tu vas* ... and then having to remember *nous allons, vous allez* ... What a perverse language, a mean language, with none of the hospitality of Arabic! "Don't try to understand, just accept it." *gn gn gn gn gn*, said the mockingbird perched on my shoulder. That night I looked up, I saw the stars in the Parisian sky. I sat on the windowsill. The cat came to rub against me and sit at my side. What can be done about uselessness when one is useless? How to be useless when others are not? Why do we say *je vais*, but we say *nous allons*? "Don't try to understand, just accept it." Just let this feeling sit beside me, like the cat. Don't chase it away, don't grab a pencil to avoid it, on the contrary. Stop fighting it. Tame it the way we'd tame an animal. Try to find the purity inside it. "Don't try to understand, just accept it." Accept? No. Learn. Learn to be useless.

WEDNESDAY, MARCH 25, DAY 9

This morning, for the first time, I woke up without feeling remotely incredulous. No thought of denying the brutality of the facts. I couldn't believe it. Until yesterday, two minutes could go by before I remembered what we are going through, and when I remembered some inner reaction made me deny the reality. I didn't want to believe it. I didn't want to accept. It wasn't possible. Until then, upon waking, lockdown and epidemic were clothes I was forced to wear, despite their rancid smell of perspiration. This morning: nothing! Nothing. Not the slightest objection inside me. It was as if I woke already dressed in lockdown. Not only already dressed, because in reality it's not a question of clothes, but it was as if, having fused with it, the lockdown woke up inside me, becoming not so much a normal state as a simple fact. Just ten days ago, what woke up with me was the reality that, after accompanying the children to school, I would take the RER to work at the theatre. But today that reality seems to have dissolved and been replaced by that of the lockdown. So then this is it, I thought, this is it, I am mutating. I have just integrated a reality that I was unfamiliar with, I am infected with the lockdown, bitten by it, and I am mutating, I am mutating like the victims in the best zombie movies. Something from elsewhere in the air we breathe these days leads us, it would seem, to those films. There's an atmosphere of invisible zombies, all the more so because the words *virus*, *contamination*, and *social distancing* arouse these irrational fears in us. Thinking about this, I am struck by the difference between the terrors that haunt our era and those in the days of Ancient Greece. Back in the time of Greek wisdom, a period much earlier than Sophocles's time, an era when there was no electricity, daylight was the greatest joy available to mortals in their lifetime. That is why vision was for them the greatest gift of all: you open your eyes and the world is there, offered, free, thanks to light. Nothing more beautiful than light, nothing greater than light, since life is short and the eternity of death sentences us to live in the world of shadows. Missing a minute of daylight was unthinkable. One had to get up with daylight and go to sleep with its waning. Always. Without fail. That is why Oedipus was considered a madman when he gouged out his eyes. It wasn't simply because he gouged out his eyes, but because in the Greek world, there could be no greater madness. He would have done better to tear out his tongue or cut off a hand. But gouging out his eyes was the greatest possible punishment! Depriving himself of light, choosing the eternity of shadows and death! It's true that there were blind people in that era, but they were usually seers, like Tiresias, invested with a vision of the future, illuminated from within by the oracular light of Apollo. But Oedipus, man among men, blind, was not a seer, he was only monstrous darkness, reviled and exiled. Condemned to wander in darkness. That's why those who encountered him saw him as a leper, or even worse, like the walking dead, physically alive but exiled from the light like the dead, one foot in life, one foot in Hades, a zombie, no more, no less. If he had to take the RER today, not only would he have to face the mistrust and disgust that has become common among travellers over the past ten days, but everyone would flee the car. And yet Oedipus learned to make the most of his blindness. Once his eyes were no longer painful, a thick layer of flesh covered the orbits and darkness became his truth. That day Oedipus fused with his blindness and from then on, he mutated. He became accustomed to it. Just as we are mutating, becoming accustomed to confinement. Even in the most difficult places, even in the homes of the men and women who are suffering a kind of double confinement, a double sentence because of the overcrowding and limited size of their private quarters, even in those circumstances, insidiously, living within the restricted space becomes a habit. The mind seeks calmness. And no matter what it takes, it will embrace habit, the only thing that brings a bit of relief from distress. In a way the reflex of habit, an often instinctive, animal reflex, could be seen as a source of comfort. In the opening pages of *In Search of Lost Time*, Marcel Proust praises the happiness habit can provide. "Habit! that skillful but slow-moving arranger who begins by letting our minds suffer for weeks on end in temporary quarters, but whom our minds are none the less only too happy to discover at last, for without it, reduced to their own devices, they would be powerless to make any room seem habitable." All that is very fine and true. But when one thinks about it, given the context, if we have to obey the doctors who tell us to remain in isolation, is it reasonable to become accustomed to this situation? Reasonable or not, many of us will obey. Habit is a virus that doesn't need to be contagious. For, although something inside me is rebelling, although something inside me doesn't want to conform, doesn't want to accept this loss of freedom, doesn't want it to become the norm, I know that I can't escape it, that I will, in turn, succumb to habit, I might even find some joy in this confinement and it is very possible that within a week or two, I will look back on this, we will look back on this, as the good old days where we were experiencing something powerful, intense, enormous, that allowed us to stay at home, together, and to reinvent time. Yes. Everything can become a source of nostalgia. Even the worst disappointments. Even the worst losses. Even the most violent situations. This might seem impossible. And yet ... During the war in 2006 between Lebanon and Israel, many of my compatriots were finally able to fall asleep, to reconnect with a kind of serenity, simply because they could once again hear the crackling of gunfire in the night. And that resembled what they had become accustomed to over nineteen years. The habit of war was so deeply a part of the Lebanese of my generation, we had grown up with it, it became so deeply ingrained in us, we had fused with our war (I use the possessive pronoun *our* intentionally, with a trace of jealous attachment, for I really consider it "our" war, it is ours and only ours, and don't let anyone try to steal it from us!), we finally mutated, we mutated with it, we mutated together. Will this mean that in the thrall of habit, several years from now we will only be able to fall asleep when something confines us? If that happens it means that this confinement today will have succeeded in trapping us, the way the civil war succeeded in trapping my generation. That civil war shaped us the way this lockdown is in the process of shaping our era. Without it, without that war, we Lebanese paradoxically feel like part of us is missing, just as the zombie would miss its death, if somehow, in order to be cured of it, that death had been removed, like the amputation of an essential organ. That is undoubtedly why I don't want to be cured of my war, I would no longer know how to speak, how to dream, without it, I would no longer know who I am, like the man who had a benign tumour removed in order to cure his spasms and who suddenly lost all the poetic sensations that gripped him, and the phantom voices he heard. In fact, it strikes me that it is through resisting the comfort of uncomfortable situations that we can remain aware, despite the pattern of habit, aware of what is happening inside us and around us and by doing this, later, we will perhaps be able to harvest things that have been sown, despite ourselves, during these difficult times. Yes, indeed, that can happen to us, that can happen to us, it can come to pass that we lose our vigilance and become accustomed to what we should detest. The impossibility of going outside and walking in the streets, of going to meet friends, that is something we should always detest, never become accustomed to. But to be frank, I don't know if I will find the strength to resist. Surrendering to habit is so pleasant. So calming. That's how I was raised, everything was set up inside me so that I would always obey the unacceptable, become accustomed to the unacceptable. And I will become accustomed to it. We will become accustomed to it. Marcel Proust's book is still there, open to the page where I copied the passage about habit that I quoted earlier. And in a moment of daydreaming, my eyes alight on this sentence: "Perhaps the immobility of the things that surround us is forced upon them by our conviction that they are themselves, and not anything else, and by the immobility of our conceptions of them." This sentence, written at the turn of the last century, appears like a thread, a thread that will help me through the labyrinth in which I placed myself, the labyrinth of habit. Escape from the labyrinth every day, if only by focusing on a new detail seen from a window. Focus more intently than we ever have on the course of a ray of sunlight on the wall across the street, regardless of how ugly that wall might be, focus on the way a weed emerges between two slabs of concrete, study, as if for the first time, the palm of one's own hand. Don't fix your gaze on things, on the contrary, let it roam, freely, over the slightest details, avoiding the pitfalls of habit, and remain, as much as possible, alive within the stone that is beginning to turn us into statues.

THURSDAY, MARCH 26, DAY 10

Driving at night has always held a unique charm for me. It feels like leaving, never to return, heading for a mystery, and the reminder that the worst thing one can do to someone is to convince them that we know all their secrets. Driving at night has its own kind of magic. It's like entering a piece of music. The music of Morton Feldman and the first movement on his album, *Rothko Chapel*. It's like throwing off the weight of things, because night devours calendars and our sense of time. It means surrendering to the twists of the road and the headlights as they reveal fragments of landscapes, for night is indifferent to the splendours of daytime. It means being free from the outside since everything is dark and at last the inside is revealed. And when we are alone, confined inside the vehicle, on deserted roads as long as life itself, an inner landscape unfolds inside us, inhabited by questions, fantasies, more or less coherent thoughts and memories. We are joined in the passenger's seat by regrets and arguments which neglect to fasten their seatbelt, and often, during these trips, hasn't the desire for reconciliation emerged as we travel away from life in the cities? Occasionally, on the back seat, the memory of past love affairs and rendezvous that never took place appear in the rear-view mirror. A cherished mouth, enchanting eyes, in the fleeting roadside shadows. Nighttime journeys can also arouse the non-events of our lives: people who never had children find themselves thinking of the children they might have had, those who were unable to practise the profession they hoped for think about how their life would have been had they practised that profession, those who didn't dare to say yes dream of turning back the clock and a thousand times, ten thousand times during the trip they repeat the yes that will never return, and those who failed to say no promise from the bottom of their heart to say no next time. As we travel the road, night unpacks our souls. Even the most ordinary nighttime trip can take on epic dimensions, become an odyssey where we imagine arriving home, even as we leave with no thoughts of returning! What a feeling of eternity in those nighttime trips from point A to point B! Perhaps because night, more than day, brings the impression of being eternal, and that's not really a false impression, or more precisely, it is a fossil impression that lies embedded in our reptilian brain, along with the trace of terror experienced by our most distant ancestors who wondered, every night, whether the sun would rise again, if the gods, or simply the mystery of nature in their eyes, would consent to reproduce the circle and once again allow the course of the round flamboyant star. All of that until one day, or one night, they discover that daytime only exists thanks to the night, and in fact, as the great Robert Davreu, a poet who knew as much about death as about light, wrote: "Night would be eternal without the night." This is an experience shared by billions of humans on earth, confined or not, sick or well. Because the night in its terrible grandeur has from time immemorial, in all eras, been the object of mistrust and a fear that we transmit from generation to generation, through it we remain linked to our ancient ancestors and we are, each one of us, the end of that line. They are here! We are haunted by the ghosts who still carry the joys and sorrows they experienced, and much of what we feel does not belong to us, but rather to them. So much so that when we are travelling alone down deserted roads, we are not alone. Much of our anger is not ours but is merged with ours, much of our outrage is not ours, but merged with ours, and we will also leave our children anger, fears, and outrage as a legacy that will merge with theirs. We are the depositories of the anger and sorrows of those who came before us, and as depositories we feel for them, believing we feel for ourselves. Or rather, something inside me that doesn't belong to me feels inside me fears that are not my own. How, then, do we separate the wheat from the chaff? The thread that attaches us to the ghosts from Before exists and never do we feel it as keenly as during times of great catastrophe. Everything becomes like the wrinkled covers on an unmade bed into which a small, a tiny earring fell. To find it, we had to carefully, gently, delicately straighten the covers, one by one, and look inside every fold. And we are still searching because what fell into those creases is so minuscule, so fragile, blending into the colour of the fabric, that we will only find it by accident, provided that this accident occurs before our death. Thus it was lost in the folds. Perhaps that is one of the key words of today, of these days. Gilles Deleuze said it so well, speaking of the French word *pli,* meaning "wrinkle" or "fold," from the Latin root *plicare,* "to fold." For Deleuze, *fold* is a rich, multiple word, *fold* is a virus that appears everywhere, contaminates everything, since everything around us wrinkles constantly. Things wrinkle, bodies wrinkle, skin wrinkles, and often souls do too, along with the ties that connect us to others. Those ties have never been as tangled in the folds as during these days that require so much more kindness and fraternity. Everything is caught in the folds of fear and impotence. Yes. *Fold* is an incorruptible word, an undividable atom found in so many of our daily words. Ex*pli*cate (meaning "to release from the fold"), com*pli*cate (meaning the opposite, "to entangle in the fold"), im*pli*cate (when we finally decide to "enter the fold"), du*pli*cate ("doubling the fold"), ap*ply,* re*ply.* Even de*ploy,* meaning "to undo the fold." All derived from *plicare*. All of this unfolds in our minds when at night, absent from everyone except ourselves, we are travelling towards a distant destination. We become the wrinkled sheets where a precious pearl, a cherished earring, is hiding. We can't find it, we search constantly, in the creases of our minds, looking for a forgotten word, a blurred landscape, a lost face, a joyous sensation. And if the covers were the multiple layers of our souls, the little earring tucked inside might be the serenity, the true serenity we have lost and which none of us, today, can claim to have found but everyone longs for. The reptilian memory in us awakes and brings to the surface of our minds fears that are not ours, the scent of bedsheets in which others have slept and which we have inherited from our ancestors. In this sense the fear and distress we feel these days, as we face the threat of sickness and death and follow the pitiless statistics of deaths enumerated daily on the creaseless screen of our devices, are not completely, not entirely our own. The fears of our ancestors who survived the plague, cholera, the multiple, deadly waves of the Spanish flu, and who buried and mourned their kin, awake in the reptile slinking through the cage of our minds. And here we are, like our distant ancestors, not waiting for day to break, but for the curves to go down, that is the image that defines my era for me. Behind every number, every day, two hundred and thirty-one today, who knows how many tomorrow, undoubtedly more, they are predicting it, I can easily forget that in reality, these are not two hundred and thirty-one deaths but truly two hundred and thirty-one humans who died. I desperately need the singular when I hear about death, the plural too easily becomes an abstraction. The singular speaks to me of another, while the plural rouses my fear for myself. The singular reminds me we are speaking of a human being like me, clinging to his life, just as I cling to mine, a human who like all human beings brings, upon disappearing, sorrow to those who loved him, just as I, if I died, would bring great sorrow to those who love me. Waiting for the curve to descend, not for the sake of those who are dying but as a sign that the end is in sight, brings little promise of great social change in the wake of this epidemic. The vocabulary of the media is a precious tool for me, it's useful because it informs me, it guides me, it helps me understand, but in this recital of deaths, it teaches me very little about the world because it wields an applied vocabulary, a polished vocabulary, free from irritants, with no creases where my mind can penetrate to feel what two hundred and thirty-one deaths in twenty-four hours really means. How can I possibly imagine the feeling of every doctor, every nurse, at the moment when a human life expires in their care? The Jewish tradition, with the tragically immense weight of experience, warns against counting humans. Dead or alive. God alone possesses the secret of numbers. When I consider how, day after day, I read the evocation of numbers as an indication of what is in store for me, with little regard for my solidarity with other men and women, I understand this warning better. The earring of compassion has succeeded today, in these times, in hiding in a fold which only those who are there, at the moment of death, can feel and under-stand. That's why I'd prefer to no longer count the dead, so I don't need to be reassured about my own fate. I would rather mourn the dead, celebrate the living, I would rather emerge from the fold where my impatience and my self-interest spin in a vacuum. And when the day comes when it's possible to go outside again, I'll try to remember this pain. And I won't go outside immediately that day. No. I won't rush outside. On the contrary. I'll wait until evening, I'll wait for the dark. And when night has fallen, along with the children, we will drive through the night to reach the sea, and there, without counting the days or nights, we will greet the first rays of dawn, and rain or shine, we will stay outside all day and celebrate life.

All day today I was inhabited by old prayers that kept running through my mind unbeckoned. Before I came to love writing, I loved praying. I liked to join my hands, focus the power of my mind, put all my heart into it and pray that whatever was distressing me be repaired, cured, saved. More than once as a child, I ran a fever, until my mother forbade me to pray. But the sight of pain inflamed everything and I saw pain as the primary form of injustice. So I'd begin again. Sometimes it was the sight of a dying cat, a neighbour in pain, a woman begging in the middle of traffic. That was unjust. It had to be repaired. Why should one person suffer and not the other, why does one die and not the other? As a child, I wanted everyone, everyone, to be spared pain and I could never bear a story that ended after a single character had been sacrificed. Praying, asking for forgiveness, seemed obvious and natural to me, like the little girl in Dreyer's film *Ordet* who asks that her dead mother be brought back to life. Of course I lost the capability of prayer a long time ago and I no longer know how to join my hands. I'm ashamed to admit that I once prayed, ashamed to admit that my first relationship with poetry was through prayer, because in the world I am part of, the theatre world, the word *prayer* has little resonance. Yet still today, especially today, the images of Lazarus rising from his grave, of the paralytic who walks again, the blind man who recovers his sight, bring tears to my eyes. And while I was still living in Lebanon, as a child, I lived with the fervent desire to be part of that. Exile in France would uproot that fervour, save me, and the stories of Jesus of Nazareth were replaced by those of Jean Moulin and the Resistance, discovered in this inestimable exile, and the verb *to believe* was replaced by the verb *to refuse*, but both *believe* and *refuse* were for me verbs driven by the desire to be worthy of goodness, the goodness that was inside me and yet had to be attained, I mean a heartfelt goodness, in other words, kindness, generosity, a willingness to make sacrifices no matter how great. Yesterday, reading the *Odyssey* for school, my daughter had to answer the question: "How would you define a hero?" After at least an hour of reflection, she wrote: "Someone who is prepared to give her life to save her friends." Children are stained, like the stain of red wine on a white tablecloth, by moments of revelation. Just as a sheet of paper that was folded will always conserve the crease, we also conserve the moment when our heart was creased with joy, with fervour. I hope that my daughter will be creased by this definition of heroism, but because that belongs to her, because she must discover the path on her own, I said nothing, I simply pointed out the spelling error in her sentence: the French word for hero, *héros*, takes an *s*. "Even if there's only one?" she asked. "Yes, because heros are never alone, because they bring with them everyone they love and defend, so that's why they are always plural, that's why the singular *héro* doesn't exist." We always turn to what has shaped us. In my case, I was shaped by the desire to someday see a statue move. Still today. I have always dreamed of witnessing a supernatural event. Fortunately it has never happened, because I think I wouldn't have survived; of all my childhood terrors, that is the one that has remained. Even today when I have to walk down the hallway in the middle of the night to reach my bedroom, or to fetch a glass of water in the kitchen, I'm gripped as much by the fear as by the hope of seeing the Virgin Mary, Christ, or simply the spirit of my mother appear before me. Sometimes, after turning off the hallway light, a few seconds of finding myself in the dark is enough to ignite my imagination, and in the time it takes to walk the few metres that separate me from the bedroom, I have time to imagine that the twin sisters from *The Shining* or, even worse, the little girl from *The Exorcist* are blocking my way. I can become so convinced that I freeze like a statue, paralyzed by terror. The presence of supernatural evil becomes so irrational, I have no recourse to reason, the only way to extinguish the flames of horror is to turn on the light again. How reassuring to find the furniture and banal objects in their places, despite their mocking chorus: "You idiot! You see? There's nothing," says the drawer of the dresser where I keep my socks, and I promptly lie down, without, however, turning off the light immediately. And yet I wouldn't want these frights to disappear, I cherish them and I can't bear the thought that I might never feel them again. They are proof that rationality has not dominated everything in me, there still exists in me, confined and isolated as I am, a dose of delirium which is, although I can neither explain it nor prove it, the only gate that can lead me to the immense garden of wisdom and poetry, the garden I am still afraid to enter, it terrifies me so. I know, however, that one day I will have to move beyond the fear that forces me to turn on the light, I will have to confront what is frightening inside and outside me, and not simply confront it, but remain there, waiting, allowing the fear to devour me, to the point of madness, the total loss of reason. Muttering incomprehensible words, I will discover a new language which will lead me to the real path of writing. It will come in time. One can't avoid oneself indefinitely. It's a kind of rendezvous with childhood, since as a child, I already wanted to see a statue move, like the scene in Zeffirelli's *Brother Sun, Sister Moon*. Faced with this impossible event, Francis screams and, suddenly trapped in a garden both magical and terrifying, he strips off his clothes, returns them to his father, and leaves the world where he was confined. That never happened to me. During the civil war in Lebanon, during an entire summer, one by one, the women in the village where we had taken refuge organized prayer meetings, taking turns hosting the others in their homes. When my mother's turn came, she'd send me to the edge of the pine forest on the outskirts of the village to gather what flowers I could find, insisting that I bring back some wild thyme and mint. I'd leave in the morning and, knowing that it was for the prayer recitals, I felt endowed with a divine mission, always, always, I could never understand why – alone in the woods, gathering wild jonquils, daisies and wisteria, big fig leaves, white stones, weeds and red earth – why a god, a saint, a spirit, a virgin never seized the opportunity to appear to me and pronounce the magic words that could have made me aware of the immense violence I was carrying inside me. And although I'd return quite disappointed by this abandonment, this non-apparition, I would nevertheless return home with the largest bouquet possible and as soon as the prayers began, boredom would overcome me. The prayers didn't interest me as much as the act of preparing for them. Is that what made me fixate on writing despite myself? After all, what is picking wildflowers for prayers if not a first act of writing? An orphan of appar-itions until this very day, I later tried to follow various spiritual paths, all of which proved to be dismal failures. They always led to the desolation described by Saint Ignatius of Loyola when he speaks of the bankruptcy of the soul incapable of connecting with what escapes it. In my twenties in Québec, and even later, I tried to practise Saint Ignatius of Loyola's spiritual exercises. All of them. I remained silent for weeks, during an entire year I avoided looking at myself in a mirror, I read the Bible and the Qur'an to no avail, nothing but deso-lation, including today, when I got up this morning thinking that this confinement resembles one of Saint Ignatius of Loyola's spiritual exercises. Sentenced to remain in the house in the springtime when the weather is beautiful for a period of six weeks, possibly to be extended, with every day the same, observing all the while the tiny differences inside oneself and resisting the temptation of seeing this as normal. Refusing to accept it, anything about it. To rebel with no means to do so. To confine oneself to confinement. Recognizing one's inability to let go, resisting, most of all, feelings of guilt, be it because others were dying and not us, others were making sacrifices but not us, because others were suffering more than us, humility, humility, and day after day, failing and starting over, remaining within one's limits, without success. An exercise to be practised without a spiritual master, other than internet and the computer, with no one to dialogue with. Desolation of the mind, confusion. Avoid falling into the stupid trap of performance, on the contrary, hear, try to hear what this is telling us. The invisible. The enemy is invisible. Everyone says so, everyone repeats it. The enemy is invisible. No, I have never seen the coronavirus in person, nor have I ever seen a statue move. Invisible. Invisible. We are shown the image of the coronavirus, like the photo of a god. And I believe I am seeing it because an authority, science, tells me this is it, this is what it looks like, just as yesterday another authority said, "This is the image of your God." But who among us has seen a single atom? Our entire world is founded on the electron, but few have ever seen one. We always believe in what we have never seen. The invisible is our lot, yet we try to convince ourselves that we are rational beings. Once this confinement is over, we will have only one desire: to resume our lives as we left them. Why should we change? Those who can go back to restaurants will go back to restaurants, those who can go back to the theatre will go back to the theatre, the economy should pick up, and it will pick up, many of us will be happy that leaving on summer vacation by air will be possible again, and at all costs, we will need to buy refrigerators and plane tickets again if we want to save our world. Wars will resume and everything will begin again. Unless, reconsidering our relationship to the invisible, realizing to what extent the invisible is the basis of our lives and our relationships to each other, we can gradually envisage a new formulation of the spirituality of the twenty-first century André Malraux had predicted some seventy-five years ago when he proclaimed that the twenty-first century will be spiritual or it will not be. To which the poet Dylan Thomas replied, "Do not go gentle into that good night ... Rage, rage against the dying of the light."

MONDAY, MARCH 30, DAY 14

"Not to be limited by the infinitely big while knowing how to remain within the limits of the smallest is divine," that is Hölderlin's very free interpretation of a fragment of the epitaph inscribed on Saint Ignatius of Loyola's tombstone. And it is also how I interpret the law instructing us not to go farther than a kilometre from our homes. "Not to be limited by the infinitely big while knowing how to remain within the limits of the smallest is divine." However. The new regulation announced by the authorities last week does not specify whether the said kilometre we are allowed should be measured the way the crow flies or not. That can be an important detail. For example, leaving from my home, less than four hundred metres south, as the crow flies, could easily lead me to Joinville-le-Pont where I find the streets much more pleasant than those in Nogent. In Joinville-le-Pont, the view of the Marne from Quai de Bethune, which runs along an island separated from land by a stretch of water, is particularly surprising. In the surrounding neighbourhood, on the narrow streets lined with lilac trees, one finds little houses, street stalls, old garages, and tiny grocery shops. Most of the streets open at the far end onto the river. In certain spots, over some one hundred square metres, there is an unexpected Venice, with small bridges and makeshift boats. Poplars, linden trees, and willows line the canal, the water is dark and dirty, and anyone who leans over it can see their reflection, rippled by the current and the fleeting passage of large greenish, slimy fish. Things here seem less cared for, less neat and tidy. Located more than four kilometres from my home, the way the crow flies or not, the Bois de Vincennes is out of bounds, so Joinville-le-Pont is where I would have wanted to walk in the time allotted by law. But not being a crow, if I were to go there, I would have to take the road the twists and turns of which push the distance to Quai de Bethune up to three and a half kilometres. Having no desire to play games with the powers that be, who undoubtedly have better things to do than to discuss pedometers and azimuths with a citizen like me, I stifle such fantasies and accept pacing up and down the gravel laneway directly behind the house. One hundred and seven steps going and, for some inexplicable reason, one hundred and two return. Five steps missing every time, like an offering to a god or a tax paid dutifully, or like alms because I was a choirboy for many years and I can't help myself, or tithing, who knows, but five steps are always missing. All this back-and-forth in the gravel laneway lined with cars occupies an hour every day in the afternoon when the children across the way aren't playing ball and the people next door haven't organized a game of pétanque. Sharing the lane among us, among neighbours, has evolved naturally, each one occupying it during the sanitary absence of the others. Once I've completed my pacing back and forth, I return home and somehow the evening goes by. Then night arrives, with its share of insomnia. Taking advantage of the fact that everyone is asleep, I allow myself a little escape and rather than wandering around the kitchen hoping for hypothetical sleepiness, I go outside again and extend my stroll a bit beyond the end of the laneway, while respecting the limits established by the law. In fact I have no need to go any farther. No. Because about one hundred metres from my house, in the bend of the road that winds its way up to the commercial street in Nogent-sur-Marne, there is a priceless treasure that, for the past year, has somehow escaped municipal inspections: a defective street light. A shadowy clearing in the middle of the city. After dark, without telling anyone, I go to stand in its halo of darkness. I look up. Protected by the bend in the road from the light shed by the street lights located above and below, I can see part of the flow of the Milky Way. This spectacle is all the more marvellous given the urban setting. Like the return of fireflies. This electrical anomaly provides a sense of reprieve. At some point, the municipal technical crew will repair this defective item, but in the meantime, this parcel of starry skies is a treat for me every night. A puddle of darkness where one's gaze can quench its thirst. And I lose myself in it often. Leaning against the stone wall behind me, there are times when I even doze off, then rouse myself immediately, startled but invigorated by this second of rest. I look up at the sky again and because, for the first time in its history, all of humanity, be it from the north, south, east, or west, is dealing with the same trial at the same time, I can feel in my very flesh the extent to which we are all part of the same tribe, despite the blatant inequities that separate some from others, the injustices, the domination of some over others, despite the violence and enslavement that dare not speak their names today, we are all in the same boat. This virus makes no distinction. Anatomically, we are all fair prey. And the more I stare at the stars in this period of confinement which currently affects two-thirds of humanity, the more I sense that we all share the same existential fear, the more I feel that my feet are placed on an errant sphere, as if I were standing on a little billiard ball shot there by accident and which travels, falling, falling in a great void, with nothing above and nothing below, since there is no one above and no one below able to sketch this immensity that has no name to contain it. And no other life for the time being than ours, in this sidereal void that a defective lamppost in Nogent-sur-Marne allows me to admire. And admire it, I do. My mind knows that what I see in the immense, dark sky on this day of confinement has taken place a very long time ago, while what is happening in this very moment in some corner of the universe, the death of a certain star, the collision of certain planets, the birth of a certain sun, all of that will only become visible from Earth a long, long time after my death, perhaps even a long time after all life on earth has disappeared. And when Earth has in turn reached its extinction, we will become in turn an ancient vision for worlds that have not yet been born. And if intelligent life emerges in one of these worlds, it's possible that one day in that world telescopes will witness the birth of our planet, the life and death of our sun. Yes. Perhaps we are merely visions in the making, and space is a roving memory. In the meantime, standing at the bend in a road in Nogent-sur-Marne, with the affidavit in my pocket giving me permission to go one kilometre from my home, I am watching the stars, aware that I am watching monsters, I am actually contemplating incredibly beautiful destroyers of planets, extinguishers of lives, gaseous infernos. So many stars, yet not one that has succeeded in supporting intelligent life like our star, a tiny little sun with nothing exceptional about it, a banal sun, a banal star compared to the grandiose stars that shine so powerfully from the most distant realms of darkness. Grandiose, yes, and yet in principle deserted, a mere playground for a permanent churning of atoms. Here I stand, then, looking up at the sublime monstrosity we call a starry sky. And its beauty cannot be denied, just as destruction and death can sometimes be beautiful. Oscillation between the infinitely great and the infinitely small. That is a paradox I came to understand very young and it has allowed me to realize that, contrary to what I had been taught, something beautiful is not always wonderful. One night I was awakened by the deafening noise of bombing that seemed to be taking place down in the valley. I was terrified. My older brother, also awakened, reassured me, saying that it was happening on the other side, that we had nothing to fear and I could go back to sleep. I got up nevertheless and went to the kitchen to drink a glass of water. There I could hear the explosions and through the shuttered doors I could see the orange glow. Curiosity got the best of me and I ventured out onto the veranda overlooking the valley. A stunning spectacle. In the dark night, I could see the trails of hundreds of bombs raining down on the villages below, shooting stars drawing thin red stripes in the dark before exploding silently at first, before the noise reached me, delayed by the distance, like the thunderclaps that follow flashes of lightning. I could see the luminous crackling of gunfire, the flaring of cannons that released a blast of bluish fragments, like glass bubbles that shatter like large insects at the moment of their cremation, zapped by the hot iron whose glow they couldn't resist. I had often heard bombs falling, but I had never attended their carnival. And what a carnival! What splendour! A spectacular immensity. Yet I had been told, and obviously believed, that nothing was more abominable than war. And there, in 1977, the year I turned nine, standing on the veranda, I couldn't understand why something so abominable was admirable at the same time. Why was I unable to take my eyes off it? I'd always believed that we had to flee monsters, that at the very thought of them, all children hide under the covers. Yet I wanted to see it all! Nothing was more awesome than the sight of falling bombs. Wide awake, I was contemplating horror with delight. I could tell that buildings were collapsing, a village was falling on its knees, levelled in a ballet of lights, in the slow motion created by distance; I could see what must have been the houses going up in flames, and above it all, the heavy thick swirls of smoke darker than the night sky. The milieu I was born into wasn't sensitive to art, I didn't yet know there was such a thing as artists, but had I known, if I had known at that age that there were people called artists and that those artists created works of art, I would've undoubtedly been sure, given the aesthetic power of the scene unfolding before the child I was, that the people responsible for this were first and foremost, certainly, artists and that war was a work of art. Nothing was as magnificent as what I was seeing. Who could create something as enthralling to watch as war, and, above all, how could such a horrible thing be so beautiful, as beautiful as the stars I am watching at the bend in a Nogent-sur-Marne road during this night of confinement? Clearly, we are wrong to trust our definitions of things. What we name is lost in space and we are fools to believe that the stars are watching over us. Nothing watches over us. And we are alone in the vastness of our surroundings. From Alpha Centauri to the stars whose only names are letters and numbers, we are always alone. We don't know where the black holes lead and we will probably never know whether they lead to anything at all. Overhead, there is nothing but light travelling through an inconceivable vastness. If that light takes eight minutes to reach us from our sun, how much time does it take from the cyclopean eye of the Big Bang? Space is a memory approaching us. That's why the distance between two points, before being a measurement, a kilometre, a centimetre, a light year, is a poem. A poem. So what is the kilometre imposed by the law of humans when a poem can place the infinite vastness of the universe in the palm of our hand? A poem says "ant" and the entire universe nestles along the lifelines in the palm of our hand. Who, other than someone who rejects the dictatorship of numbers, can hope one day to know his number?

TUESDAY, MARCH 31, DAY 15

Today the wind had risen and forced me to climb onto my neighbour's wall to prune the tops of the bamboo swaying violently, threatening the power lines leading to our house. After a few awkward attempts, armed with a bread knife in lieu of pruning shears, I managed to hoist myself onto the narrow ledge of the wall and stand up. I began edging towards the bamboo that was still six metres away. Standing, trying to ignore my vertigo, I began to put one foot ahead of the other. Suddenly, looking around me, I had the feeling the sky was opening up and, with the wind, the sensation that I was flying. The sky was so blue it was drinkable, and for a few seconds the sense of confinement was gone, undoubtedly because there on the wall I felt a sense of unexpected freedom, all the more unexpected because it came, I admit, with an activity that I'd been dreading (I should have pruned the bamboo weeks ago) – and for no obvious reason, no obvious reason, and with no idea what made me think about them, I thought about my friends and I experienced more acutely than ever the full weight of this situation we are trapped in. There I was perched on the wall and my thoughts turned to my friends, gratuitously, for no reason, as if the gusts of wind could only speak to me of them, remind me of them. And yet it's not as if we see each other that often! Even without the lockdown, I rarely have an opportunity to see my friends and I've become used to living separated from them, even used to finding some happiness in this separation. And there, standing on the wall, I felt a great sadness come over me. Not for my friends, not for the lockdown, but for all the people in mourning these days. What could be more natural than to feel sad for others when we start to think about our friends, because friendship understands gratuity, a gift bestowed expecting nothing in return? I have never demanded anything of my friends, just as they have never demanded anything of me. Neither thoughts, nor presence, nor proof of friendship. I did walk along the wall and prune the bamboo but I don't remember doing it. I simply know that back on the ground, I saw that the bamboo was pruned, after which, like yesterday, like the day before yesterday, like tomorrow and the day after tomorrow, the hours were spent doing the usual household tasks, and not for one second did I cease to think about my friends and about our friendship. First of all, and this is an important detail, my closest friends are not all artists. Far from it, and although there are relatively few of them, they are very different from each other, they have very diverse professions and many things separate them: personality, temperament, opinions, interests, to such an extent that I hesitate to introduce them to each other, worried that they wouldn't appreciate each other and that they would fail to see in each other what I find so exceptional in each one. The impossibility of bringing people who are dear to me together doesn't make me sad, on the contrary, I cherish their strong temperaments and their real shortcomings that make them the lively, special individuals they are. When I think about my friends, I am perfectly aware of their shortcomings, but these reinforce my affection and make the friendship I feel for them all the stronger. Is it, in any case, possible to be friends with a person who has no shortcomings, a perfect person, if such a monstrosity even exists? What would be the point of a friendship with a perfect individual? How aggressive, how suffocating it would be to have a friendship that forbade us to make the slightest mistake, forced us to mask all our failings to be worthy of this perfection! That's why I love my friends' shortcomings. They prove that it is neither for the sum of their qualities nor for their lack of shortcomings that I like them, but rather for how totally incomprehensible yet marvellous they are. Will we ever understand why we become attached to a precise reflection of the sea or to a person's profile? Will we ever understand why we become attached to the light in someone's eyes? Will we ever understand why, occasionally, for no apparent reason, our heart leaps with happiness and we jump for joy? Who would insist that we tally qualities or shortcomings in these magical moments? And so it is with the friendship I feel for the few people whose faces came to mind, as if printed on the blueness of the sky, while I was standing there on the wall in the breath of the cool wind. Their shortcomings are part of the landscape, they reassure me and indicate that I am not unaware of theirs, nor they of mine. But regardless of their differences, regardless of their qualities and their shortcomings and the circumstances of our meeting, these friends have in common something that I lack, that I admire, and that I envy: a detachment and an unfailing correctness. They also share a gaze that evokes travel, a gaze that seems preoccupied by something else, something inexpressible, always elsewhere, and it is this gaze of theirs that moves me most deeply. Circumstances and life's commitments make it impossible for me to see them as often as I'd like for the simple reason that they live for the most part in different countries, and aside from the lockdown, even in normal times when we are free to move around, free to come and go as we wish, we only see each other when one or the other has travelled to the country where one or the other lives, and although we remain in touch, connected, in thought, by letters and moments of intuition, there are some of them I haven't seen for several years. Strangely that is also part of the equation. Standing there on the wall, immobile, as birds flew back and forth, freely, over my head, it struck me, without knowing what it meant or whether it's a mere coincidence, that it is much easier for me to get along with people who live at least five hundred kilometres from their parents and their place of birth than with those who live two hundred metres from their place of birth. Perhaps it's a coincidence, but when it comes to my friends, aside from the taxi driver whose situation comes with the most extraordinary story, these are individuals geographically distanced from their place of birth. Of course I'm not dogmatic about this, but I realize that my friends are almost all foreigners, all speak different languages and prefer everything that is strange to what is familiar to them. Standing on the wall, thinking of my friends, I knew all the neighbours could see me, I sensed some of them standing at their window, undoubtedly wondering what I was doing standing there, immobile, like a cat in the sun. Did they guess that I was there, like a man who'd found a crack and decided to defy confinement? I don't know, but that's what had just happened to me and I was determined to make this impression last as long as possible, like a man who, not recognizing the room where he finds himself, briefly thinks he's back in his childhood bedroom exactly as it was, and while he rationally attempts to re-establish where he truly is, he tries to make this vivid sensation last a few seconds longer! And to retain this feeling of being outside, this feeling of freedom without my residence affidavit in my pocket, I called upon my friends and imagined that I was with them. And here they are. Here they are. The DJ for example, the woman I call the DJ and who is so close to my soul, I haven't seen her for close to six years. She is undoubtedly as busy as I am, and several months can go by and suddenly, who knows why, I receive a message from her, always musical, always sung, sent from a destination where life, work, love, or who knows what led her. Unaware of her whereabouts now, she could be anywhere, I decide that she is in a village in the south of Lebanon where she once wrote me from. I see her walking down a lane lined with olive trees, returning to her confinement in the home where she is teaching French to the children of a Shiite family. But on her way, she passes an enclosure, an old church, an old mosque, it's hard to say, now a stable, the DJ enters, finds the acoustics divine, sits down and hums an Easter hymn, like that, an offering to life, to light. Of all my friends, the

DJ has the most tender, the gentlest most loving heart, of all my friends, she is the one who truly believes in angels. I am with her now, sitting beside her, snuggling close to her and her song whispers in my ear. I say her name, she says mine, and I know we are together. Her song ends, she says goodbye and leaves, making room for the great vagabond, for the man I call the great vagabond, with deep affection since I owe him all the words read and written, all the words I have read and written throughout my life. The vagabond, to whom I owe everything. Of all my friends, the vagabond is the one who prefers to sleep outdoors. Ever since I've known him, that is, since the last century, he's always been looking for a flat roof where he could spend the night, and he likes nothing better than to know that he will wake up with the morning star. Right now he is sitting on the roof of his tiny room, facing the lagoon that leads to the ocean, at the end of the island of Sri Lanka where he has been in confinement for the past two weeks, where he spends his time making, with the colourful paper he finds in the stationery stores of Mumbai, Kolkata, or Chennai, minuscule collages that are as lively as Nicolas de Staël's paintings. You see, the vagabond has chosen a path that bypasses writing, a path closer to the colours of painters, although words remain his faithful friends because he, the vagabond, despite himself, is loved by words like Ulysses of yore was loved by the gods. I join him on the roof. Seeing me he laughs, as usual, his way of expressing affection, and as I sit down beside him, he says, but for no apparent reason, these words that are his, "Sometimes I think that the universe is full of lost secrets. That even secrets are destined to get lost and the chance of finding a secret is reserved for the one who knows how to keep it." Night falls on the vagabond who falls asleep, not so much to enjoy sleep, but to prepare for the surprise and the joy of awakening with the rise of the morning star. This way of being is the exact opposite of the taxi driver. The taxi driver is Greek. I met him during a trip to Athens and we have remained friends since. Confinement has forced him to park his yellow cab and right now he is practising the trumpet, since the taxi driver has an ear for music and sometimes, between customers, he stops by the sea, on the far side of Piraeus, and starts to play. Now he is lying down in his small apartment listening to music. I knock on his door, I've come to visit, he opens the door and we sit down facing each other although we don't have much to talk about. The main point with the taxi driver is not conversation but the simple fact of sitting there together. The taxi driver is laconic. The faces blur. I am back at home. I sit down. I look out the window. Life goes on. It goes on, but I feel more acutely than ever that my friends, the DJ, the vagabond, the taxi driver, and others, the Japanese friend, the American bear, the Polish philosopher, the collector of placemats, the Great Rolland, the photographer, the actor-baker or the family-hater, all of them, all these friends, guide this life that goes on, like the Polar Star reassures the sailor who, lost at sea, suddenly sees it shining through the magical scattering of the clouds. Then, searching my phone for a message sent some two years ago, I find the DJ's song when, at Easter, she began to sing in that deserted enclosure, singing simply because the acoustics were beautiful. Listening to her this evening, she is the voice of the friendships that found me on the wall and moved me to the verge of vertigo.

WEDNESDAY, APRIL 1, DAY 16

A dung beetle, he is pushing up the hill an immense round stone that constantly rolls back down, lower each time, just as he thinks he might succeed; sentenced to an eternal punishment, he descends again, only to resume his ascension, gasping, snorting, pushing the heavy stone up to the summit of the hill where, again and again until the end of time, he will have to go back down, then resume the climb. Such is the painful fate of Sisyphus according to his myth. In the perpetual resumption of our days, more and more identical, it could be tempting to see in the image of Sisyphus the comical, cartoonish images of the likes of us in confinement, little imitation Sisyphuses, struggling up and down, from morning to night, under the weight of time, our stone that grows heavier as the sea of our situation seems to carry us to lands that appear more and more hypothetical. "When will we reach the Indies, Christopher, when?" Columbus's crew asked him as he stood at the ship's rail and he, staring into the dark, had no answer. Since we know there is no longer a New World, how we can hope that the crossing of this confinement will lead to the discovery of a new continent? But Sisyphus is more than his stone, Sisyphus is also the hill. This makes it possible to imagine that, on the contrary, Sisyphus decides to drop the stone, since what really interests him is less the solution to the equation than the desire to identify, in the itinerary that leads from the bottom to the top, where, at which infinitesimal moment, the mistake takes place, the wrong move that will cause the stone to roll back down just as the summit is within reach. Sisyphus searches avidly for this moment, he searches for the pebble which, in this immense itinerary, will overthrow, reverse everything. A pebble? No!

Not even a pebble. Sisyphus is looking for the grain of sand, the invisible dot, the inert, inconceivable dot, he is looking for the virus that will cause everything to collapse. Like Sisyphus, as I dwell on our situation, morning to night, going around in circles, up and down, I keep thinking about the moment when it all began, when in total anonymity, the virus that has placed us in confinement was transmitted to the first human being. Thinking about that, I can't help but wonder where and at what moment the tiny error happened. How can that moment be identified? In order to understand. How to find that first human, find that fateful instant which has isolated us, sentenced us to discontent, and for many of us, to idleness? Apparently one day in November or December 2019, somewhere in the city of Wuhan, here or there, an infinitely tiny thing happened between the animal world and the human world. A transmission, a tiny grain of sand under the foot of the stone roller, causing no disruption, no upheaval, no noise, a silent infection that has toppled everything today. "And the Lord God commanded the man, saying, Of every tree of the garden thou mayest freely eat: But of the tree of the knowledge of good and evil, thou shalt not eat of it: for in the day that thou eatest thereof thou shalt surely die." And we all became subject to death. So from what tree have we eaten to see disease spread across the earth as if it were precisely knowledge whose fruit was forbidden, the knowledge the myth of the Garden of Eden warned us about? What is so dangerous about knowing, Sophocles once asked in the desperate cry of the Queen Deianira in *The Trachiniae*. "Queen, do not rush towards knowledge," her friends seemed to warn, "Queen, don't seek to know what will destroy you!" But oblivious Deianira, eager to know her downfall, wants to know what is killing her and, tasting the words that name her downfall, just as Eve ate the forbidden fruit, she has no choice but to hang herself with the rope of this knowledge that she wanted to see despite the danger, banning herself from the garden of life, like Lot's wife turned into a pillar of salt, Orpheus turning back to the fated Eurydice. What prevents us from practising restraint? What drives us, and then what is so dangerous about knowing? Today we clearly have the answer. Not only have we tasted the forbidden fruit, we have devoured the entire tree, bark and all, we have devoured Paradise, we have devoured God and reduced the world, again and again, devouring, swallowing, eating. One day, somewhere, here or there, an infinitely tiny thing happened between the animal world and the human world. It all comes down to that. That could be the first sentence of our collective novel. And like any first sentence of any novel, no matter how you look at it, all these first sentences say the same thing: one day, somewhere, something happened to someone, and the novel consists of telling the story of what happened. So how will the story of the novel we are writing unfold? And has this novel already been written? The answer to that question isn't so obvious. When we start reading a novel for the first time, we are holding the entire story in our hands before it begins, and just because we have only reached page 32 doesn't mean that page 76 doesn't exist. Page 76 is already there, in our hands! And if, without our knowing it, only on page 166 will everything take a tragic turn for the hero we are identifying with, page 166 is already there, waiting for us, and page after page we are irreversibly heading for that page. It is there, the tragedy is there, it pre-exists. Is it possible, then, to imagine that that day in November 2019 in the city of Wuhan, like page 166, was something that had already existed for a long time and that we were simply moving towards it? And if Wuhan was page 1, does page 378, which has not yet happened in our lives, already exist at the heart of the book time holds in its hands? In other words, are we predestined? Or does everything come down to chance and coincidence, with no meaning, no direction? I cannot answer that for myself, one way or the other. Everything seems written, and yet I like the freedom chance offers. In fact when I think about that first person in Wuhan, I could become so angry and refuse to think of him or her as my fellow human, and in doing so repeating a circle that has existed for a long time. But in the case of chance, I can rethink all that, I can think about Cain and Abel and tell myself that had Cain decided to be his brother's keeper, rather than acting so smart, today we would have a different relationship to violence and bloodshed. I could also imagine that it would have taken very little for that first person in Wuhan not to be contaminated. If, for instance, his or her walk had been interrupted by a conversation with a friend, if, for one reason or another, they had decided to head in a different direction, they wouldn't have been infected. The flapping of a butterfly's wings, the terrifying chaos theory! This is chaos, born of the flapping of a butterfly's wings on the other side of the world. But in quantum mechanics there is also the idea that at any given instant in Time, any event can have multiple outcomes, they all occur even if we only experience one of them. So that theoretically, at this very moment a parallel world exists where that first person went in a different direction and wasn't contaminated, meaning that in that universe there is no lockdown and the name of the coronavirus is still unknown. I close my eyes and think of this world that exists, I think of us humans in this other world, at this very moment, sitting at tables in sidewalk cafés or walking down the street, hugging each other, greeting each other, totally unaware of what our world, our parallel world, is going through. I think about this parallel world born of the possibility that the first person wasn't infected in order to lift my spirits. This means the men and women who died of this sickness are over there, on the other side, in this parallel world, still alive! And out of friendship for this other me, I can be happy that he isn't going through what I'm going through. This kind of fantasy has often come over me. And although I'm not proud to be carried away by such delirious thinking, I can't help but remember all the ifs that have marked various turning points in my existence. If this, if that, if we hadn't, if he hadn't, I wouldn't have been there, and if, if, if. It must be said, these are major ifs. For instance, my father, at the start of the civil war, with his usual precaution, had procured for each of us, my mother, my sister, my brother, and me, five visas for five countries that he was careful to renew every three months, in case we had to flee the country from one day to the next. And when that one day to the next occurred in the summer of 1978, my father sent my brother to the man who acted as a travel agent in our village with instructions to buy five plane tickets for the first departure for one of the countries for which we held visas. "Well, sure ... but ... which country?" my brother asked. "Whichever! You take the first flight to one of these countries." My brother left, and during his absence I could hear my father, my mother, and my sister juggling suppositions and prognostics based on our five possibilities: France, England, Italy, Egypt, or the Ivory Coast. It was like musing, in the summer heat, which sauce we would be eaten with, and when my brother returned, we looked at him, wondering what our sentence was, and in the silence of that sweltering summer, my brother simply said: "Paris." Knowing today that we spent five long years in Paris, that I learned French there, I have often wondered: what Italian might have I become? What kind of Ivorian would I have been? What Englishman? Where would I be today if the flight schedule of Middle East Airlines had chosen another destiny for me? Is it pure chance or was it written? And then, five years later, after the most grotesque scene, sick, diagnosed with cancer, desperate, unhappy, my mother was thrown out of the Paris prefecture station, having been told that our papers would not be renewed, that our time was up, we had had our share of French generosity, and that we had to leave the territory within three months, and there, once again, the game of Russian roulette resumed. Aiming for the city of Houston, Texas, where the climate resembles that of Lebanon, and because, to quote the sentence my mother kept repeating, "Americans aren't like the French," saying "French" the way one would say "idiots," we got used to the idea that we would certainly settle in the US, like Khalil Gibran, the true icon of Lebanese literature, a century earlier. Then, at the last minute, with a law decreeing that any Lebanese family about to arrive in the United States with children twenty-two years old or older would have to leave these children behind for a year before they would be allowed entry, and my sister having just turned twenty-three, the American dream crumbled. That was when Montréal appeared as a last resort, the only solution, Montréal, with the friends who were already awaiting me, with the theatre already awaiting me, with great love stories and winters I couldn't begin to imagine. Was all of that already written, or was it chance? What hill is ours, from which summit, as we constantly roll our life up and down, will we seek to identify the tiny error, the virus that contaminates and often robs life of carefree moments and joy? What grain of salt so often thwarts happiness? What invisible cat will trip our steps? And if, in truth, Sisyphus only pushed his stone up the hill once, but passing through all the parallel lives that were his, going up and down constantly, his malediction consisting in exploring all the possibilities that were his, everything he might have been. That is undoubtedly the hell where Zeus wanted to imprison him, the man who wanted to defy death. That is undoubtedly when it's the uniqueness of our lives that makes them bearable, even if they are often subject to twists of fate. Often we think, "I wish I had lived another life, I wish what's happening to me wasn't happening," but perhaps it's these very events that will determine that the stone of our life will only reach the summit of the hill once. It's the fact that our life is only one, never multiple, never duplicated, that allows us to look inside ourselves, like into a vase where all dreams remain possible, unhampered by all those what if this, what if thats. The uniqueness is what allows us to cross the most arid deserts.

THURSDAY, APRIL 2, DAY 17

Over the twenty-four years I lived in Montréal, every spring
I made note of the exact date when the trees in front of my
house began to bud. From year to year, the date varied
between the sixth and the ninth of May. In the very different
climate of Lebanon, the trees begin to bud in early March, two
months earlier than the trees in Montréal. Two months every
year, for twenty-four years. Adding up those months, I come
to a total of some forty-eight months, in other words, four
whole years. Four less years of greenery in the course of my
life. Confined at home now for almost three weeks, I am
thinking of those lost months, those months when the snow
kept on snowing in Montréal, while outside my window in
Nogent-sur-Marne, I can see that the trees are budding and
the tender green has appeared already. This association of
ideas is undoubtedly what triggered the sadness I feel today,
a debilitating weariness born of boredom and despondency.
This is beginning to resemble those endless winters in Québec,
I thought. It reminds me of the eighth of November when
the inhabitants of Ilulissat, on the west coast of Greenland,
gather one last time to salute the sun that won't reappear for
another six months. With one real distinction – as interminable and taxing as the winter can be, the Québécois know
that spring will return, since it has never failed to return,
century after century. And the inhabitants of Ilulissat aren't
worried as they count the days, because they trust the order
of the heavenly bodies and they have faith that the sun will
obey this order and will reappear behind the icebergs on
April 16, at around two o'clock in the afternoon. But we,
on the contrary, have no certainty. And without any certainty,
undoubtedly like so many others around the world, too

discouraged to muster the energy to do anything, I suddenly found it impossible to believe that this confinement would ever end, nor could I imagine a reason for it to end. How can this ever come to an end? We will be confined in perpetuity. So, determined to shake this torpor, this useless discouragement, I picked up a meat cleaver and tackled the task of defrosting the freezer compartment whose door no longer closed because of the accumulated layer of ice. What a disaster. I had to stick my head inside the freezer and work fast so as not to lose the frozen food I'd stacked on the kitchen counter, and there, with my head surrounded by artificial snow, my cheeks burning from the contact with the ice, suddenly my vivid memories of waiting for the bus at minus thirty in Montréal came rushing back. To each his own madeleine, and mine was a freezer. And there, enveloped by its cold, as if encased in it, I recalled the Montréal alleyways where I often went walking, and the unfulfilled dreams and hopes I nurtured back then. The Berlin Wall had just come down. I was twenty-one years old. I believed that the world was still the world of yesteryear, the world of the Resistance, the world of Albert Camus, of Václav Havel, of Jan Patočka. But despite everything, despite these names so meaningful to me, it was a time when I felt the world was trapped in the middle of an interminable winter, undoubtedly because of the unending civil war in Lebanon and the many other crises my family had faced. In a way I was happy collectively and unhappy personally. And the only way I could find a bit of light was to leave the house and go somewhere, anywhere. I especially enjoyed exploring Montréal's alleyways in the middle of the night. Walking down those alleys made me feel protected, and I liked the solitude they provided. Less well-lit, more neglected, left to their own devices, alleyways have a conviviality that streets don't offer. On the contrary, I remember finding the streets overwhelming with their shops, their cafés, their trendy bars, their restaurants, and their crowds. The streets, especially those frequented by groups of young people enjoying their youth in a way that escaped me, were violent reminders that a social life is only accessible to those who succeed in life, those who have the means to pay for the array of riches available to satisfy our every whim. That meant that the streets confronted me with my mediocrity, my failure, my incapacity, and the humiliation of feeling that all that merriment – those girls and boys who seemed so carefree and were so well-dressed, who looked so sure of themselves – all that would clearly remain beyond my reach in those years when I was so far from success, be it social, scholastic, or professional. I was so far from having any positive sense of myself that I went around in a fog, without realizing it was a fog. That is why I preferred the alleyways where I could escape the bright light that reflected my mediocrity. Of all the North American cities I had the occasion to visit during those many years, I can affirm that the most beautiful alleyways can be found in Montréal. I often explored them at night, because I found nighttime at home unbearable. I'd leave the house, whether it was raining or snowing or freezing, and I sought peace in the gift of my legs, and the art of putting one foot ahead of the other, until the act of walking absorbed me. Many things come to us through our feet. These things can take years to reach our head, where we suddenly grasp what that wandering meant to us, although the longest distance, yet to be covered, is the path from the head to the heart. No one can reach the end of that path without passing through many trials. It takes the harsh trials of loss to reveal a human being's true worth and to lead him to his centre. If it's true that at the moment of our death, we see our entire life pass before our eyes, I will see the interior landscapes I visited for years on end in the snowbound alleys of Montréal. Night after night spent walking in search of ... I didn't know what. Just because paradise is lost doesn't mean it doesn't exist. Always walking, setting out on a journey, immobile or not, and knowing that – no matter what, although the objects might be inert, reality unchanged, although a stone will always be a stone – there where we least expect it, will come the quiet tread of the angel. Knowing that means living like someone buried alive, preserving our dignity, and forcing ourselves, come what may, to see in even the tiniest insect that comes to visit us in our grave a sign that life is present and that we can still be rescued, that it's possible until the very last moment. Perhaps that's what is painful. Sometimes we have to reach the point where we've lost all faith before the hand that will retrieve us from nothingness can appear. Life can't be reduced to a simple exercise in lucidity. It requires more. To hope without hope. To wait without waiting. And to accept contradictions, to go so far as to allow contradictions to guide our walk: this foot, yes, that foot, no. Vision is born of two contradictory movements that come one after the other. And I lived in that contradiction, feeling more at home in the alleyways than in the streets. Especially at night, especially in the winter. In the winter the alleyways look even wilder than usual. They reveal the strata of different seasons. The alleys that run behind the houses in Montréal offer a more intimate view of people's lives because they overlook their kitchens, their backyards, the sheds where their bicycles, their outdoor furniture, and their old cars are stored until the following spring. All buried under such a thick layer of snow the idea that it might melt someday seems totally absurd. The alleyways run parallel to the streets they're named after. While in the streets, we can meet cars and people, in the alleyways we always meet animals. Cats and dogs, of course, but also grey, bushy-tailed squirrels and large crows, heavy and black like witches, and occasionally, under a pile of wood or cardboard, families of raccoons. One freezing night in the alley behind avenue Coloniale I found myself face to face with a coyote I mistook for a wolf. I froze, terrorized, in the biting cold, not daring to move. We stood there looking at each other. The wolf stared at me, then turned away and I watched it amble off and disappear behind the huge snowdrifts, beyond the halo of the street lights. That was in the early '90s, before the wave of gentrification, back when Plateau-Mont-Royal was a working-class neighbourhood and students could still rent relatively spacious apartments for two or three hundred dollars a month. From avenue des Érables where I was living, between avenue Laurier and boulevard Saint-Joseph, I struck out every night and walked all the way to the Old Port in Vieux-Montréal. It was an hour-and-a-half walk that, during the winter, lent itself to fantasizing. Following the network of alleys, going from one to another like a voyageur travelling from stream to stream, not having to worry about cars or passersby, I could surrender to the stories and the dreams that haunted me. I lived countless love stories with girls who were completely inaccessible to me, I lived a thousand heroic adventures where I saved the world, died a thousand times, and a thousand times over I pronounced my own funeral oration. These fantasies shaped my way of thinking, and to a certain extent I became so completely wrapped up in them, I forgot the cold, I forgot Montréal, I forgot all my troubles and I really became what I saw in my fantasies: a lover, a hero, or someone who died for the sake of humankind. A cheap meditation to overcome the feeling of mediocrity and to pre-serve some reason to go on, a reason to get out of bed, morning after morning. And somehow, without realizing it, an hour and a half later, I'd reach the waterfront and a place beyond Marché Bonsecours that no longer exists today, where I could contemplate, from the embankment where I stood, the dizzying power of the Saint Lawrence River one metre below me. The Saint Lawrence. Absolute power, a slice of azure storm fallen to the earth, the entire arm of a continent where whales come and go, sacred river that flows from west to east, from the Great Lakes to the Gulf, far away, beyond Newfoundland, filling the ocean, and already in Montréal, where it's considered narrow, one can barely see the opposite shore. The Saint Lawrence. The Saint Lawrence River was the expression of everything I felt churning inside me, every-thing I didn't know how to express: anger, desire, rage, and an insatiable longing for the infinite. From this observation point that was so dear to me, I could also contemplate the Jacques Cartier Bridge, reclining Eiffel Tower that connects Montréal to the South Shore, an immense iron dragon perched on its powerful pillars, holding fast in the current of the river. There, the sky was even vaster and the river even wilder. I often said to myself, "At least I will have seen this, contemplated this. At least I will have experienced this in my life." With the wind that never failed to blow over the open expanse of the river, the range of temperatures was impossible, an abstraction for someone from the Middle East like me: minus thirty, minus forty. Temperatures that drive you crazy, intoxicating temperatures that make you want to eat the crystallized air suspended over those fields of maritime waters, freezing the retinas of your eyes. In those moments of extreme cold, the tragic appeared marvellous. You could simply close your eyes and, standing there on the embankment, wait to fall asleep. Dying of the cold is so good, so sweet and so marvellous. To rebecome a statue, like those statues I wanted to see move in the Lebanon of my childhood, so far away from that embankment. And there at the very end of an adolescence that hadn't been easy, having lost my mother tongue, having even lost my mother, I often tested my desire to live. It was deeply rooted. I had no children, no commitments at the time, and when I really thought about it – after the double exile from Lebanon to France, from France to Québec, after the violent deaths that had marked those painful years, and the many disappointments I nurtured about myself – I couldn't find a single reason to resist my temptation to put an end to it all, especially since it would have been so simple to climb over the wall there and simply let myself slide into the comforting power of the Saint Lawrence. I know the river would have embraced me immediately, its currents are so immense, its gigantic arms impervious to the mediocre lives entrusted to it. Of course I would have felt a moment of panic the instant I entered the water, but that moment of panic would have been insignificant compared to the depression weighing on my heart. Child's play. There it was, a low wall standing between me and peace. But no matter how often I said that to myself, no matter how I clearly I knew it, no matter how ardently I longed to end it all, like so many adolescents choose to do despite the sorrow it will cause, no matter how often I ticked off the points that made me an ideal candidate for putting an end to this struggle, something metallic, immutable, made me realize that I would never cross that line. Why? It was neither fear nor dread, but the conviction that it simply wasn't me, as if someone else were whispering in the ear of my twenty-one years: "No, that's not you." Because I toyed with my life several times in that city and it was there that I understood that my fate was to live, I loved Montréal like I've never loved another city, I've never been as faithful to a territory as I was to Montréal, and I've never been as attached to any territory as I was to Montréal – although I know that I would never want to live there again. I took my head out of the freezer and I could see the river, the way it bursts through the ice floes in the springtime and we can witness the reawakening of its power interrupted by the dagger winter drove into its heart. Like a wild beast breaking free of its bonds and reclaiming the fluidity of its strength, the river resumes its course to the sea, like a life beginning again, a life that seemed to have died, extinguished forever. As I looked outside the window in Nogent-sur-Marne and saw the sun setting, I thought of that. No matter how long this winter we are experiencing lasts, we must be a river, with the power of reawakening bound to return.

FRIDAY, APRIL 3, DAY 18

I want to beg mercy from this day that's beginning. Ask it to pass like a caress on the forehead of each and every one of us and protect all the people who see it dawn. Ask it to meet with death and convince it to pass over for once, convince it not to be needy and to put its handiwork aside; may the day find arguments for death to grant a reprieve to the men and women it intended to visit today. And if, like the knight returned from the Holy Land, the crusader in Bergman's *Seventh Seal*, it dedicates the day to a game of chess, we could suggest that its partner be Philippe Jaccottet, our greatest poet. In him death would find its most powerful adversary. Death would have someone to talk to. And while the knight of the last seal needed to know, before dying, if life had meaning, if God existed, and if the plague ravaging the world was the apocalypse announced in the Gospel, Philippe Jaccottet, much more formidable, would move his first pawns, and rather than waxing eloquent, he would speak to death about the colour of poppies. And I quote him:

So many poppies growing among the weeds.
Red, red! [...]
Too gay for words [...]
All these almost transparent dresses, barely fastened, quick,
quick! Sunday is short ...

And if death, facing such a daunting warrior, refusing to battle, also refuses to grant a reprieve to those meant to die today, then may this day, donning its most brilliant, most lively light, accompany death to the bedside of the dying so that the people who will die today may close their eyes without fear. To this day that's beginning, I would like to speak words that will express our distress, even if that will change little in its course, and tonight, when day is done, many more of us will leave. But what words can be found? I have neither the art nor the means to shatter reality, and I lack the talent for words that might strike their target and appeal to this day that's beginning. I play every card in my hand so it will hear me. All the songs of the world. All its beauties, its cathedrals. But will that be enough? Near the village of Huanchaquito-Las Llamas in northern Peru, where the Chimú, one of the greatest pre-Columbian civilizations, once lived, the remains of some one hundred and fifty children sacrificed in a ritualistic ceremony were found. Researchers believe that these one hundred and fifty children were sacrificed when devastating floods, caused by weather patterns of El Niño, ravaged the Peruvian coast. A true catastrophe for a society largely dependent upon its harvests. "They probably wanted to offer the gods their most cherished possession, and that was their children who represented the future," explains Gabriel Prieto, the archaeology professor at the National University of Trujillo who conducted the digs. Is that what this is all about? In the film *The Sacrifice* by Andrei Tarkovsky, in the face of the nuclear catastrophe that has destroyed the world, Alexander, the main character, undertakes the same sacrifice as the Chimú and promises God he will sacrifice what is dearest to him if the world can rebecome what it was before. Like the Chimú, Alexander believes in the power of the word and in the power of promises. Tarkovsky's film proceeds accordingly until the end, for the day after his promise, Alexander will lose everything dear to him, and the world will be saved in return. What about us? Are we prepared to sacrifice everything dear to us to put an end to this disaster? Or do promises and words only taste of politics and communications today? Are we simply waiting, confined to our homes, for things to resume being as they were before? Without any real sacrifice on our part? But what could we sacrifice?

And how to believe that sacrifices could lead to anything? So go ahead! Why don't you go ahead! Sacrifice what's dearest to you, instead of talking about it. What sacrifice could you make to ensure that this day that's beginning is a day sent by life? What's to be done, what action can be taken so the wind will rise and we can see our ships set sail again? Doesn't the story say that no sooner had the priest passed the blade through Iphigenia's throat, releasing not the vermilion red of delicate poppies but the scarlet blood of youth, than the wind rose and carried off the rapid ships of the Greek armies bound to destroy the towering walls of Troy? Isn't that what the story says? Agamemnon sacrifices his daughter, a sacrifice he would pay for dearly, since, soon after his return home after ten years at war, he will be decapitated, axed to death by his wife Clytemnestra, still mourning the sacrifice of her daughter. But Agamemnon is just a legend, some will say, and sacrifice has metaphorical meaning in a story. Indeed, but he wasn't a legend, many people knew him, the man who, in the middle of Paris, returning to his bookstore, saw the Gestapo arrest his son, and so that nothing would be lost, no name be given, no place revealed, father and son, seeing and recognizing each other from afar, agreed in a glance to remain silent, and immobile in the bright sunlight of that day, while the SS patrol raised their rifles and took aim, father and son both knew the sacrifice being made was more important than this moment of gunfire, and even after his son's blood had been shed, his body lying on the street, the father had to pretend to be indifferent, as if that body meant nothing to him. Isn't that the price that was paid to win the war? And us? What about us? Well, now. Here we are after almost three weeks of lockdown and something seems to be saying that, in fact, we will have no pity for each other. None. The mistrust in the air, as soon as we set foot outside, is only the smallest of symptoms. And how can it be otherwise? When I think of the marvellous world I was living in, so comfortably, so happily, undoubtedly the likes of which few generations before me in history have known, the world that allowed me to become who I am and to live freely, how can I accept the loss of that freedom and comfort? How not to do everything to recreate that perfect harmony when that world, for the past forty years, day after day, constantly, forcefully, strove to convince me that it would be infinitely more useful for me to purchase a dishwasher than to cultivate a sense of courage and sacrifice? We no longer need to be courageous, I was told, and I was all too happy to believe it! The peace treaty has been signed, I was told, and I believed that, too. We no longer need to sacrifice anything: we are beyond the age of sacrifices, sacrifices are the superstitions of ancient times, to be buried at all costs. And here we are, brutally confronting the promises we didn't keep. Yet they were simple promises: anyone facing the uncertainty of life will be helped by the rest of the tribe. The simplicity of that promise. No one will know poverty. Everyone will be able to pursue their aspirations. A promise enshrined by law. And this was taught in all the schools, these promises inscribed on the façade of our institutions. Liberty, equality, etc. All that was written, decreed. After our massacres, after the unspeakable, with great pomp and circumstance, we made a number of promises which peace, comfort, indifference have led us to break, calmly, serenely, one after the other. Now, today, with little true sense of what the word *promise* can mean between us, with few words kept, other than the one that says to others, "Mind your own business," we stay inside our homes, and many of those who die, die separated from their next of kin. That's where we stand. No one to speak gently to the dead. No one will be there today to whisper in the ear of the dying the final comforting words we all deserve. You are about to cross the valley of death, you are going to die, that is what's happening, you are going to die, you're afraid and that is normal, but I am here with you, I love you and I am speaking to you, I am speaking to you, my daughter, you, my son, you, my father, you, my companion, you, my friend, you, my brother, you, my little sister who is dying before me, you, my grandfather, you, my great-grandmother who took care of me when I was little, singing me the old-fashioned songs of your youth, you, my master, you, my secret, you, my heart, you, my soul, you, I will guide you and guide your journey down the dark road. You are dead and if you can still hear me, use my voice as a road to travel into the heart of the luminous night that awaits us all, and because I, still alive, I am speaking to you, you will not stumble on this road, because I am speaking to you, you will not be afraid to lose your way, and on this last day of your life, you will know now and after this life, how much I love you. That is what we are not able to do. Nor can we open the windows once the last breath is taken and let the wind enter. No. We remain sitting in our houses. So how to respond to this? Obviously, the response must be the antithesis of death. Birth. *Birth* in the real sense of the word. Because, concretely, pandemic or not, every day thousands of children are born around the world. Concretely, every day, and this day that's beginning will be no exception to the rule: thousands of powerful lives will be born, will come out of their mother's womb. Each one a living being, a soul, a new beginning. Today. Now let's imagine the men and women who will be born today in some twenty years. Let's imagine them asking us questions, and because they will be twenty years old, let's imagine that one of the questions these marvellous children born today, on this eighteenth day of confinement, will ask will sound like this: "What did that extraordinary experience of the lockdown change in you, Papa? What did it change in the world, Mama?" We will undoubtedly say that it led us to review our health-care system, that it encouraged every country to take charge of everything essential to its survival. But if, insisting, some of these children ask for more details, perhaps we will say that it resulted in a lot of literature, many marvellous movies, a lot of essays, a lot of thinking, many great plays and a huge awareness of our fragility. Imagine that, of all these children who will be born in a few hours, along with this day that's beginning, just one, boy or girl, insistent, asks again: "Mmm, fine, okay, that's great, but I mean, profoundly, what did that change for people, personally? How was it before the pandemic and what did it become after? Surely you can't impose confinement on half of humanity without having something change fundamentally? What did it change? What did it change?" If this question were to be asked by one of the children born during the coronavirus pandemic, how will we answer? How to answer this child in whom we are trying to inculcate the humanist values of sharing and solidarity, this child we want to see succeed at school and socially, this child who was given access at school to literature ranging from Homer to Jaccottet, including along the way all the philosophers and poets, this child into whose head we kept drumming the grand principle of democracy, who was forced to memorize the Universal Declaration of Human Rights, visit the museums on slavery, the Mémorial de la Shoah, this child to whom we harped on about the need to fight the exploitation of our brethren, how can we answer that, no, essentially nothing changed afterwards? Emerging from the lockdown was complicated, we remained a bit traumatized, but basically we carried on like before. How can we answer that, and especially, how, having answered that way, can we dare ask that child to go on believing that words and promises made can still have the slightest value?

MONDAY, APRIL 6, DAY 21

Curled up behind the sofa, confined, one might say, in a space that only he can reach, showing just enough of his head to keep an eye on us, the cat is mystified. He watches us from there, one round yellow eye staring at us. "How come they're here all the time?" he seems to be wondering. For him, the slightest change is a source of concern. Not all changes worry him, however. The ray of sunlight that slips down the wall and across the floor, only to fade away at nightfall: he's familiar with that; he can measure its geometry throughout the house and he knows the puddles of light, here in the morning, there in the afternoon; and the clouds that filter bright daylight, he's familiar with them, too; and us, with our comings and goings and our alternating presences and absences, the silence and the commotion they cause, that's familiar, too, but the relentless permanence of our bodies seems to appear to him like the oracle of the gods appears to a human being: incomprehensible and undecipherable. An enigma. And judging by his behaviour, it doesn't seem to make him happy. It's almost as if he's sulking because we're always here. It must be said, as Jean Cocteau wrote, that unlike dogs, there is no such thing as a police cat. And *Felis catus* enjoys being alone from time to time. Cats are animals who think first of themselves, while dogs think of the pack, and with few exceptions it would rarely occur to a cat to risk its security to help another. Altruism isn't a cat's strong point, and the thought of a master who should be obeyed isn't part of its genome. For cats, that's nonsense. It's less a question of egotism than a way of viewing the horizons of existence that this sensitive creature has developed. For a cat is sensitive. People who have never had a cat have never been struck by the delicate manner cats have when they come to snuggle against us when sorrow and sadness drain us from head to toe. That doesn't mean that cats are empathetic, no, but with their love of stability, they detest changes in mood and will do everything to soften them, and just as they hate to see us unhappy, they can only moderately appreciate our moments of excessive happiness. If *Felis catus* were a climate, it would be as moderate as possible. That doesn't mean that cats are asocial, not at all, on the contrary, nothing is more companionable than this meditative creature for anyone who knows how to observe the rippling of its fur, the arabesques of its tail, the infinite variety of the positions its ears can take and of the hues that can shade its eyes. And should anyone still doubt the bonds that exist between *Felis catus* and *Homo sapiens*, it should suffice to notice how, unlike dogs who bark to communicate with each other, cats never meow to communicate with another cat. They growl, they hiss, they howl, but they never meow to each other. The cat's meow is reserved exclusively for humans! Of all the animals, cats are the only ones to have adapted their expression to ours, and it isn't absurd to think that meowing is their attempt to imitate human language. Learning from us, cats meow to us the way we talk to them, they meow to us like someone speaking a language they haven't totally mastered, like children who, wanting to imitate a foreign language, simply imitate the sounds. Getting close to us through language, cats bond with us, become attached to us. But in their own way. Cats like the presence of life, and when two humans are having a conversation late at night, in the conviviality of nighttime, cats will often come closer and lie down, purring, basking in the warmth of words spoken in friendship. And they will stay there as long as it pleases them. That is happiness for them. Cats are happy as long as they know they are free to leave when they wish. Aren't we like them, and don't we also wish we could leave the house when we want, to come and go as we want, owing no explanation to anyone? Choose to be there or choose to leave. Dogs whine pathetically as soon as they are separated from their master. And while it is possible to create a bond with a dog and go so far as to train them, sit, lie down, stand, attack, this idea seems crazy to 99.99 percent of all cats, and I wish good luck to anyone who is determined to get a cat to fetch a stick thrown at a distance. The cat will react with boredom, before yawning languorously and turning away. And while a dog, indefatigable in this game of go-fetch, couldn't care less about variations provided that he's confident his master will stay nearby, cats cannot tolerate a shift in their reference points, and the slightest variation in the organization of things can cause depression. That is the cat's weak point. A piece of furniture that has moved, a change in the colour of a wall, a mirror that breaks, these can constitute a major upheaval. Without being observant, a cat is like those photosensitive cells on which the various, surrounding realities leave an imprint, and developing these imprints inside her, the cat produces a photo which, fixed, frozen, becomes the framework that ensures her equilibrium. This fixedness allows the cat to integrate, down to the second, the time at which each one of the humans who share her territory will wake up, and although the notion of time remains an obscure notion in her mind, she knows when this one or that will leave and when they will return. And this external regularity becomes the mirror of her internal regularity. Hence the enormous mistrust the cat we live with seems to have developed towards us since the beginning of lockdown. He looks askance at us. Hour after hour, from one evening to another, we are still there! From morning to morning, we no longer leave the house. We have turned his habits inside out. And as if wanting to adapt to this confusing situation, no longer sleeping in his usual spots, he goes back and forth, from room to room, from one bedroom to another, on the lookout, as if sensing our confusion, the cause of which escapes him. A blue cat of the Chartreux breed, he never meows for no reason, he "thinks" twice before speaking, and since I've been writing this diary at night, he sits in the doorway and watches me for a long time, something he has never done before. He goes round in circles in the children's bedrooms, watching over their sleep, standing guard so their nightmares are not too terrifying. There's a threat in the air, but he only senses it vaguely; thanks to his discomfort, of which I only became aware a few days ago, I also became aware of the effect this lockdown must be having on how animals see us. For animals have been watching us since time immemorial and they measure their existence against ours. Be it the ants that have invaded the kitchen or the spiders weaving their webs in the room where I work, they know how to remain discreet. They only go about their business when we are looking elsewhere. They are always keeping an eye on us, we are there in their minds, their ears, their senses, their antennae, and they know we are universal predators. They have no illusions about us. And their caution towards us goes well beyond our homes. Last year, at the same time of the year, I heard the robin trumpet its first mocking notes around three o'clock in the morning, taking advantage of the deserted streets. These days, it waits until five o'clock, as if the pressure were off and it could enjoy sleep a bit longer. And farther away, in the streets of Paris, the pigeons are confused as well. "What's going on?" they coo. No one is in the streets, the bread crumbs are few and far between and the garbage cans are empty. Poor pigeons, it hasn't been an easy year for them. First they had to survive the municipal policies with the introduction of crows and ravens in their airspace that made their life impossible. Many of them died of hunger, many saw their nests raided by these predators more powerful than them, and now today they have to fight the rats who, forced out of their hiding places despite their immense mistrust of humans, appear in broad daylight, looking for food, stealing anything to be found that's edible. Ducks are straying farther and farther away from the places where they were fenced in, and coyotes have been spotted roaming closer to downtown Montréal. Every city can report on disruption in the animal world and its surprise. Wild animals, everywhere, everywhere, inhabitants of the rivers, the forests, of all the usual territories, are emerging from their dens, while we live in confinement and always the same startling question: "What is happening to the humans?" Horses, butterflies, river rats, and all the wild animals who have always been quicker than us, sense well before humans imminent catastrophes, earthquakes and tsunamis, volcanic eruptions and typhoons, and stay put in their trees, in their fields and meadows; Nature remains silent while humans become frantic. So this can be their opportunity to take advantage of our panic, our confusion, the trap we have fallen into! But they do nothing. Why don't they unite to take advantage of our reclusion? They must know that for the last almost thirty years, in Europe alone, in order to feed, clothe, heal, and embellish 751 million inhabitants, we have to slaughter one million living creatures an hour. One million an hour: pigs, hens, chicks, cows, calves, bulls, cattle, and fish, all varieties of fish, worms for fishing, shellfish, crabs and lobsters, crayfish and even periwinkles, lab mice, experimental frogs, ducks, rabbits, and deer, and everything that crawls on the earth, swims in the sea, flies in the air, the rhinoceros for their horns, the whales for their oil, the tigers and the beavers, and everything that gallops, the bees and the locusts, all of that, we need a million an hour! One million of their kind. Why wouldn't they take advantage of this situation? An eye for an eye, a tooth for a tooth, and we could see wolves, bears, rabid dogs, and poisonous snakes, we could see all the winged horses of the legends, Pegasus and Xanthos, invade our cities and enter our homes to destroy us, assisted by the horde of birds, from eagles to buzzards, from crows to falcons, from chickadees to barn swallows, a swarming much worse than in the Hitchcock version. They could do this, but they don't. My cat has just come into the room and jumped on my table, and sitting down, he looks at me. He looks at me and I look at him.

Without turning away from me, he lets out a soft meow. I ask him: "What?" He meows again. I pat his head lightly. I ask him: "What's the matter? What's going on?" He looks at me.

"Don't be so worried," he says in perfect human language, and I'm so frightened my heart skips a beat and freezes. "Listen to me. No wild animal wants the extinction of humans. No animal wants to dominate all forms of life the way humans do."

"Is that because you animals see hope in the future? Are you waiting for the day we will attain more wisdom, a better comprehension?"

"No," he replies, "we are not waiting for anything, hoping for anything, we have no expectations, since waiting doesn't exist for us. In order to wait, you have to believe in the future, and that's the last thing we would want to feel."

"But you animals can foresee disasters."

"No. You're wrong. We are here. We sense how terrified you are, and we don't wish for a disaster."

"But why, why?!" I ask him. "Why do you have pity on us?"

"You're wrong again. Animals have no pity for anything, and when I chase a fly, I kill it, when I catch a bird, I kill it, and I do the same with a mouse, and I know that should a wolf appear and catch me, he wouldn't take pity on me, he'd kill me."

Then the little cat comes closer to whisper in my ear.

"Listen ... Listen, human, listen carefully. Seeing what will happen in a minute or in a thousand years has nothing to do with the chain of events. We animals pay little heed to causality, and if a bird sings, it's always because another bird, hiding in the shadows, is watching. Every animal who chooses visibility chooses for another who is hiding, and every animal who dies dies for another animal who remains alive and hides. We are the visible doubles of an invisible world. Listen carefully, listen to the animals' secrets: for us, unlike you, the future is in no way a necessity. Do you want me to tell you what the future is? The future is a closed box where madness dances with a razor blade. Back and forth they go, in a frantic, unending waltz. Even if that could produce an awareness of the future, it would be crazy to intervene because anyone who tries would be butchered, and they would become aware of the future and the future is always, always, painful. And no creature desires this pain, except for humans. Because they are already suffering from this madness that no animal possesses. Joining this dance, human blood flows and this flow of human blood offers the other forms of life time, and its continuity. If human blood ceased to flow from the box of the future, all life would end. Someone has to be sacrificed. Blood must be shed for time to go on. Human blood is the slime that allows the snail to move. That is why, for us, animals, despite all the harm you do to us, despite the piles of animal carcasses, despite the extinctions and the suffering you inflict upon us, your existence remains precious for us."

The cat left, landing heavily on the floor. He turned back to me and meowed, encouraging me to follow him. He was hungry, his bowl had been empty for a while. I fed him, he rubbed against my legs, I patted him, he ate, and he left to lie down between the children's bedrooms, standing guard over their dreams. It was five o'clock in the morning. I opened the window. The dawn of this twenty-first day of confinement was breaking. In the immense silence of the sleeping city, I suddenly heard the mocking song of the robin. And I knew, clearly, that this gentle teasing was meant for me and me alone.

TUESDAY, APRIL 7, DAY 22

Distressed by how early I woke up this morning, I cursed sleep, I cursed the pillows, I cursed the paint on the ceiling, and I didn't even want to take my shower, a blow to the hot water, hoping to prove that I was still, occasionally, capable of a certain kind of rebellion. To prove it to the entire bathroom, from the toothbrushes to the Marseille soap bar, made in Bangladesh, I weighed myself, and I swear on my mother's head that I looked at the numbers that appeared on the scale's cathodic screen with total scorn. I barely got dressed, refused to change my socks. Since it's impossible to stage a rebellion while staying at home, may as well attack the drying rack and the squeaky doors. "What's going on, what's wrong with you?" the toilet and all the plumbing that goes with it asked cheerfully. "What do I know, I don't know, that's how it is, I'm losing it, I'm blowing a fuse," I answered, "I got up on the wrong side of the bed, and I've got a right, I have a right, you hear me?" and I flushed the toilet, hoping to end this argument which, I could tell, would lead nowhere. I thought I was special with my bad mood, but realizing a bit later that everyone in the household was in a foul temper, I decided the best solution was to go round in circles, which I proceeded to do for a long time, going so far as to change a light bulb that hadn't even burned out and measure my children's height, despite their protests, I'm the father around here and, dammit, there's a reason why the word *despot* comes from the Greek *despotēs* which means "master" and by extension, "father." They didn't get slapped, because it's against the law, but they did get two centimetres more each, and that seemed to please them. After this unexpected euphoria, two centimetres (sometimes it doesn't take much, but this much can be hard to find), I decided to organize my backpack, which I hadn't touched since we went to war, three weeks ago, and despite everything, my backpack seemed considerably more serene than me. "Now you shut up, too," I warned it, hoping to make things clear, "I'm in no mood to put up with your smug attitude," and I unzipped it, and unzipping it, I came face to face with my appointment book. "Hello, here I am," it said with its usual sardonic chuckle. "It's me! Do you recognize me? Your agenda! Luke! I am your father! Do you remember me? It's me!" Then I understood, yes, like Skywalker in his epiphany, that it, my agenda, calling upon its dark powers to jolt me awake, was what had led me there. After being sentenced to the dark, it was responsible for my mood. "So this was a trick to lead me to you. You schemer!" I said. Without answering, a simple provocation, like a lightsaber that flicks on and aims its deadly ray, it flipped open and promptly turned its pages until it stopped, of its own accord, on today's date. Dire mistake! In big red letters, in my own writing and underlined with two pretentious strokes, two words strode across the page: "SPRING VACATION!" Devastated, I broke down and came to the painful realization that today I was not where I intended to be. It's true. Today was the day we were supposed to leave. Train tickets, rental car, little house, all of it gone with the wind. Like everyone else. Too bad. Tomorrow morning, when I wake up, the tides will have no importance and the dunes in Sainte-Marguerite will be more deserted than usual. The lighthouses will rotate their cyclopean rays in the dense night of Finistère, with no one to appreciate their shining in the dark, they will be as useless as windmills with no wind, and the reefs of Aber-Benoît, offshore, in the distance, just before the great ravine of the ocean, blind and insensitive to the caress of the waves, will have nothing to capture in their jaws: no hull, no boats, no ships, not a single sailor to devour, nothing. Easter vacation. What a farce. The flight from Egypt won't take place today, and as for the Resurrection, we'll have to wait. In a few hours, Jewish families around the world who, over the centuries, have had reasons to hide, will once again recite the story of the Exodus from Egypt. "Why is this night different from all other nights?" "Because plagues were brought upon the people of Egypt, but the pharaoh refused to listen to reason and continued to persecute your ancestors." "The plague, what plague?" one of the children might ask, "the coronavirus?" "Worse, my child, worse, because the first-born were smitten in great numbers and the waters drowned countless valiant warriors and your ancestors wandered in the desert for forty years before receiving the Law and returning to the Promised Land." "But aren't we still in confinement? Will this ever end? Where is the promise of this land if we are still confined?" "Yes, you're right, but is the promise always what we think it is, child?" And certainly unsatisfied with this question in the guise of an answer, impatient, the child will search for the afikomen while in neighbouring homes, children will be searching for chocolate Easter eggs, unable to understand how the bunnies, given the drastic public-health regulations, managed to enter our yards, even inside our houses, and well into the back of our cupboards. The bunnies have been vaccinated against the virus. "Oh, really? And Jesus?" "Well ... what about Jesus? Jesus rises from the dead and leaves his grave." "What do you mean, he leaves his grave? He doesn't have permission to leave his grave! We are in confinement. The president said so: no exceptions!" Quite true, this year things have taken an unexpected turn. In fact, things have been taking unexpected turns for a long time. Something no longer exists and will not recur. He took the bread and broke it and gave it to his disciples saying, "Take, eat; this is my body, given for you." "Ummm, that won't be possible, Rabbi," Matthew, the most legalistic of the twelve will say, "that's against the distancing regulations." So Judas will have no need to betray, nor Peter to deny, nor the cock to crow, or if it does, it will be for naught. That's how it is. It's no longer necessary to associate Easter eggs with a story. What matters is the availability of the eggs, there at the patisserie, open exceptionally. Easter eggs, explained the helpful salesgirl, are considered essential goods as we approach the Easter holiday. Regularity in the spiritual justification of our purchases: February 14 is the celebration of love, roses, heart-shaped chocolates, and dinner in a restaurant; Easter and its eggs; Mother's Day and its roses; Father's Day and its neckties; followed by summer and its thongs and throngs of tourists; Halloween and its candies; Christmas and its myriad presents, and the cycle repeats itself. Disney, year-round. With these two words in red, my agenda plunges its lightsaber into my heart and I feel as if I'm dying, so I close my eyes and I remember the dunes in Sainte-Marguerite at the northernmost tip of Brittany. Simply saying their name calms me. In their sandy lap, it's so easy to indulge in marvellously useless musings. There in Finistère where nothing, neither the wind nor the waves, need be silent, impossible to wade towards the patches of diaphanous grey light at low tide without sinking in the shiny silt left by the tides. The horizon in Finistère is different from other horizons because we can see its curve. When the foam in the tide pools farther out glitters in the streams of sunlight, we can feel the roundness of the earth, we feel that we are on a sphere, we feel that there we can walk towards Land's End and that beyond lies the magnificent blue nothingness, streaked as if with jumbo markers overflowing the lines, the boundless lines that reach you, reach your tongue that can taste the ink and inspires in you a thirst for the boundless, always, all the time. If blue can be that blue, then I can write impossible sentences! In North Finistère, not far from the dunes in Sainte-Marguerite, we can walk to fuzzy islands where hares and turtles run wild, where we collect countless stones, like little treasures we will discard later, we bury the carcasses of innumerable crabs, and we build and destroy a series of ever more sophisticated sand castles. Sometimes I walk off, leaving behind the two little builders I love with all my heart and I allow myself to float in the breath of the wind. Focusing on my geographical location, I locate the north, east, south, and west, and visualizing Brittany, then France, then Europe and Asia, I travel until my thoughts reach the other side, the opposite Finistère. Vladivostok. Every year I entertain this daydream, thinking of the day when I will leave these dunes and walk for two long years to reach this other extremity. This thought makes me feel so exuberantly alive! I am resurrected and I escape from Egypt all at once, I stand up and I stare at my agenda who, thinking I was dead, was preparing for its victory! I haven't died yet, I stand up and I look at it. "You are no longer all-powerful, Agenda! The dark side is visible in you, but you still have much to learn about the Force." And I head towards it, armed with my happiness that travels from Finistère to Finistère, and on the pages of the dates that follow each other, I see everything that had been so pretentiously inscribed in this notebook of time. I see the excessiveness I had bought into! This schedule, steeped in all these things I believed I had to do, that I considered urgent, important, crucial. All these people I ab-so-lute-ly had to meet, with whom I im-pera-tive-ly had to speak, all that evaporated, erased, crossed out until further notice. What notice? Who still wants to give notice? And why should I obey such a notice? What if this confinement allowed me to see the possibility, as utopian as it might be, of time that no longer moved like an arrow I have to follow, but like a journey? My agenda, guessing my intentions, understands that freeing myself from the constraints of time, I am freeing myself of it, and faced with the danger my freedom represents for it, it begins to fight back: "You won't have any choice," it says, "because you'll have to work, and I'm the one who controls your work, me, your agenda, your time. Without me, you are reduced to nothing! You can't get along without me, since, you loafer, you haven't reached retirement age yet and just as Javert only frees Valjean at the moment of his own death, I won't let you free yourself from me until the day of your retirement, which will be, duly and surely, dictated by the law. And it will be inscribed in your agenda!" But I don't reply to these arguments, or I reply with scorn and I open the big atlas and I begin to plan my journey: dunes in Sainte-Marguerite – Brest – Landerneau – Paris – Nancy – Baden-Baden and from there, find the source of the Danube and follow it, Passau, Ybbs an der Donau, and then Bratislava, where I'll visit my friend Kristina with a bouquet of her favourite flowers and then resume my journey, passing through Oyor, Budapest, without lingering, continue and a month later reach Timişoara, go to the theatre, say hello to the actors and travel on again, always travelling on, beyond Romania, circle the Black Sea in the north, Moldova, Ukraine, and having reached this point, make a detour via Yalta, in memory of Chekhov, then head for Kazakhstan and its rolling plains, waiting there for winter to end, before approaching Mongolia in springtime. Often sleeping outside, following the Russian border and crossing it at the most northern point of Mongolia, avoiding North Korea and then finally, exhausted, undoubtedly reduced to silence which will be a new version of prayer, and my memory stripped of everything, having forgotten even the word *theatre*, perhaps no longer even knowing how to write, I arrive in Finistère East, and there perhaps simply sit down and laugh, laugh, for at that point I will realize that not once during this journey had I thought about my return. The day ended when my son came to wake me up, his hand on my shoulder like the hand of an angel. "Papa. Can we look at the photos from last year's vacation?" "Of course." And we opened the shortbread-cookie box, bought two years ago in the Landéda bakery, the box where we keep our jumble of souvenirs.

WEDNESDAY, APRIL 8, DAY 23

The room where I write is rectangular. Two of the walls forming one angle are blind. The other two, forming the opposite angle, each have a window. The first window, behind me when I am writing at my desk, faces north, and the second, to my right, faces west. The wooden floorboards are eighteen centimetres wide, the walls are white and hold three shelves for books and notebooks. The table is made of a slab of the Amazon rainforest, fallen from heaven. The varnished wood has veins of forest green, khaki green, some yellowish veins, and a line of vivid mandarin orange that runs along one of its edges. There is a cast-iron radiator on the wall behind me. Against the opposite wall, in front of me, a cot. Of everything that makes up this space, what I cherish the most isn't the windows, the objects, or even the door, but the four corners of this rectangle. Although they are all in this one room, and this rather small room creates a uniform impression when you enter, all four corners are very different from one another. And each one creates a very different sensation. That reality gives me constant pleasure and I'm very attached to the differences that distinguish the four corners of the room where I work. I find nothing more depressing than a room made up of four identical corners that create the same impression. I have the unbearable sense of being a prisoner in a world that has lost all depth. And yet the few people who for one reason or another enter this room notice the view from the windows, they comment on the special table, they're interested in the books lying around, but rarely, if ever, do they notice the diversity of the four corners, although I have deliberately accentuated it. There is a wastepaper basket in one corner. A globe all children find irresistible in an another. In the third, a motley arrangement of stones collected in various places, snail shells, wooden matchboxes filled with the bodies of dead insects, feathers from crows, pigeons, chickadees, magpies, and even one vulture feather. And in the last corner, more or less thrown on the floor, illustrations, photos, pages of random notes and drawings beside pencils, the pencil sharpeners and wood shavings, erasers, scissors, glue ... I pay little attention to what is on my table, even less to what is on the shelves, but nothing in the four corners is left to chance. In my mind the corners of a room are like human beings. We need to listen to them carefully. After fifteen minutes of a filmed interview Peter Handke had agreed to do with me in his garden, he made it clear that he'd had enough and it was time to eat a kabob at the corner restaurant. "You can leave your things inside and we'll leave," he said. "Go ahead, go around the house and you'll see a door out back. Go in and leave everything there." And after a brief pause, as I was headed with my things in the direction Peter Handke had indicated, he added, "That's where I write." I'll never know why he felt the need to mention that. Was it because he'd sensed that I was interested in writing? I don't know. And I don't think he knew that I write. So why? A touch of vanity because he must have sensed my admiration for his work? Or was it simply because he'd understood how important it was for me to enter clearings where the voltage is well above the usual vibrations? And epic writers like him know how rare these clearings are, how the ivy of daily reality tends to strangle everything and how precious it is to find these surviving spaces. He was offering one to me. I entered. A small table where twelve perfectly sharpened lead pencils were lined up like soldiers. A chair where hiking clothes lay in a pile. And although I did take the time to count the twelve pencils, I noticed all that when I entered, but I quickly turned away from the objects to crouch down and examine the spacing of the floor tiles and the exact spot where the base of the table was placed on the floor. I examined the places that few people examine. And knowing that I'd never have this opportunity again, at least not in these circumstances, in this context, I dared approach each of the four corners of the room. I closed my eyes and listened carefully. Not one of the four told the same story. There was the murmur of something different in each one. Crouching there, my heart racing, frightened by the thought that someone – who? writing? – might discover me, squatting in the dark like a thief, I heard the breath of the books that had been written there, in that room, books that had moved me so deeply. In the third, the most confined of the corners, the darkest since it was farthest from the sources of light that entered through the windows of this small, low-ceilinged room, in this third corner, entire passages of *My Year in the No-Man's-Bay* – which will always be one of my favourite books – came back to me and I felt as if I was sitting in its ink. Every writer who writes, writes from a cave. A corner with no concealed door, where the sentences seeking their page bleed like a stream flows to its river. Crouching in the corner of the room, deaf to everything else, I could suddenly hear the open wound of injuries and disappointments, the sorrows and the rages, as well as the great, sublime life force that inhabit this author. I could hear this clearly and I had the feeling that I'd come closer to the true nature of his book. I couldn't linger any longer, I walked out casually, as if nothing had happened, and we left to eat kabobs with Alain Françon, who had arranged this meeting for me. I didn't mention any of this to Peter Handke. Not only do I do this with places, I do it with people as well. And often when someone is talking to me, my mind wanders and I start to listen not to the words, but to the voice. I try to listen to the cave from which this voice is trying to escape. I listen as if this person were a room where all the patterns of their writing live. So while the person is speaking to me, I go from corner to corner, noting the differences, although it is one and the same person speaking to me. Likewise I know that I myself am many in the polygonal diversity that constitutes me. And I couldn't bear to think that the world, or anyone, could reduce me to a single angle, define me in terms of a single corner, as real as that corner might be. In this respect, worse than confinement, worse than imprisonment, the sentence of which our society has become the uncontested champion, the reduction of an individual to a single angle in the eyes of the world and all networks, is the most painful, the most terrifying of all punishments. A person who feels defined by a single corner – the corner of the wastepaper basket, the garbage, the filth, the crime – no matter what that person does, he will always be sentenced to being nothing other than that error, with no chance of being anything other than that corner of suffering. That is undoubtedly what Franz Kafka's "In the Penal Colony" is about. A colony where a machine engraved the sentence and the judgment in the very flesh of the accused. The diversity of the corners that constitute us is one of our most precious attributes. That's why I'm so fond of examining all the corners of a room. Noticing their differences reminds me of how the human mind conceals so many multicoloured, diverse, and varied corners, often contradictory but belonging to the very same mind. Not just belonging to it, but constituting it, shaping and anchoring it. I lacked that capacity for listening for years. For years I heard nothing. I deeply regret that no one taught me sooner to pay attention to the corners of places and people. If I had known how to listen more carefully, if my mind had been better trained, if my soul had been more ardent, if I had allowed Bach's sonatas to enter my heart rather than trying to understand them, if I had been more patient, patient enough to overcome the moments of boredom that I often succumbed to, if I had been less riveted to the me inside me, hiding, trembling at the thought of disappearing, I would undoubtedly have been better able to hear the prophetic words addressed to me on many occasions. Like that day, standing in a Métro station in Paris, when I asked Souha Bechara how, having attempted to assassinate General Antoine Lahad of the South

Lebanon Army, firing two bullets at close range, she had managed to survive ten years in the Khiam prison, the detention camp the Israeli army had built in the south of Lebanon so that Lebanese could be tortured by Lebanese. How did she do it? This woman who for ten long years had been held prisoner in a cell measuring a metre and a half long by a metre wide. Ten years. If nothing else, how did she manage to maintain her sanity? That day, on the platform in the Métro, in her quiet, melodious voice, Souha Bechara replied: "I simply had to think of the reason I was sure I'd be killed and that revived my dreams. You know, nothing is more powerful than the conviction you can have about life." Souha – who sang when in the cells next to hers, women and girls, men and children, were being tortured – Souha was already telling me what I couldn't hear. She was saying, "Listen, don't let anyone say after you have left, 'That solemn-eyed boy is leaving, he wasn't generous, his heart remained closed.'" But there in the Métro, at that moment, I didn't understand the words of my sister, heroine among all heroines in my heart. So today, motivated by the desire to do a good deed and to listen to the words of another person, to explore the corners and listen carefully to the nooks and crannies of a stranger, I dialled a random number, trying a 01 number first, then a 02, then a 03, and it was finally someone from the 04 area who answered. "Hello?" "Uhhh, yes, hello ... uhhh ... listen ... we don't know each other. I dialled this number by chance. This is not for a survey or for any particular reason, I simply wanted to have a conversation with a stranger. I'm beginning to miss talking to someone I don't know, just speaking to them, speaking to someone. So if by any chance you have time, we could, I don't know, just chat for a few minutes, since we're all going through the same thing." After a brief silence, the man invited me to call the helpline available to people experiencing psychological distress or depression, and he promptly hung up on me. Life doesn't contain the same heroism as books. And besides, what does "heroism" mean

these days? In my case, over the three weeks of my confinement, alone in just one of my multiple corners, I realize that
the very notion of heroism has dissolved. Really. I look at
the nature of these past three weeks. What a strange experience we're going through, an experience that makes everything
else appear dull. It's as if, for years now, slaves to the dictates
of our realities, we hadn't really lived. Actually, I can't remember. Have we really lived? Before the virus we had moments
of life, each in our own time, each group in their own time,
each movement in its own time, but what have we experienced
together? The women's movement remains, inalterable, yes.
But the virulence, both of its expression and its reception,
shows that it has not yet attained its point of clarity. But
otherwise what was there before? Does anyone remember?
And why is it that today, thanks to this horrible virus, despite
ourselves, we feel the powerful pulse of life that vibrates inside
us and irrigates all things? So what was missing for us to
need such a dire situation to feel this power? What terrible
wind is blowing? What is this epic movement if not a powerful
wind urging us to be heroic, but what kind of heroic?
Undoubtedly heroic in a new way. In a modern way, a white
square on a white background, a urinal, everything that
resembles us, since we're dealing with heroism without heroism. Where no one is expected to act courageous, because
unlike everything humanity has always espoused ... from
Ulysses to Spider-Man, from Aeneas to Joan of Arc, from
Captain Nemo to Marie Curie, who all sacrificed their lives
in their lone battles against society, solitary but illuminated
by the power of their mission ... Unlike them, our heroism
lies in our refusal to risk our lives. That is contemporary.
No matter how hard I search or probe, I can't find anything
in the ancient myths that remotely evokes this kind of bravery:
No matter what, *do not risk your life.* In all civilizations and
in all eras, there are the tales of daunting trials, lost dogs
who courageously find their masters, monsters to be beheaded,
evil spirits to be expelled through exorcism, tales of Martin

Luther King Jr., Jean Moulin and the Resistance, Antigone. Far from us. So are we something else? For us heroism does not mean being the chosen one among an immense, anonymous crowd going about their ordinary lives, but our heroism is the heroism of community, fraternity, where the individual doesn't seek to be different from others. Not even those others who vote against our candidate, those who live different lives according to very different values. Our heroism lies in the challenge of accepting to be exactly the same and to do the same as everyone else, that is, *nothing*. So ...? What's bothering us? That over the past seventy-five years we have found nothing to share, nothing in common, except this virus? And what if now, taking advantage of this opportunity to finally come together, as if listening to the same corner, we took a quantum leap for once, the same leap at the same time, together. If that is possible, if that is possible, then perhaps, without realizing it, we might be about to discover something immense. Let's just look at the moon tonight. Raise our heads and look up. It's the full moon on this the twenty-third day of confinement. A full moon. Is it possible that, like Copernicus's realization that the earth revolves around the sun, we might be on the eve of an even greater discovery? That, as inconceivable as it might seem, something is pregnant with us? Something is carrying us in its belly and is waiting to give birth to us? Yes. We are in a belly and we understand that we have just turned and the time has almost come for us to be born to something. But to what? And how? How are we going to be born?

THURSDAY, APRIL 9, DAY 24

According to a book on everyday objects I found in a bookstore in Prague in 1994, the first mirrors were created in the Anatolian region six thousand years before our current era, using volcanic obsidian stones that when naturally polished reflected a dark image of the face. In Prague I was living in the only habitable apartment in a building under renovation at 15 Cimburkova Street. In exchange for very reasonable rent, I was taking care of a cat named Stalin and some fifteen plants. I knew Prague well, although I had never set foot there before, thanks to Franz Kafka's novels, his diary, and my collection of biographies and illustrated books about him. Many period photographs showed the houses where he had lived, his father's shop, and the cafés where he met with his friends. On one map of the city, I had reproduced the itineraries he could take from home to work, so when I arrived in Prague one July morning, I was disoriented by the fact that the city wasn't in black and white like my photos, but very colourful with its pastel façades in shades of pink, green, yellow, and even red. It was in that city that symbolized so much to me, in that unlikely apartment, that one evening, with Stalin purring on my lap, thumbing through the marvellous dictionary of everyday objects, I read the history of the mirror and realized that this object hadn't been conceived by nature. Although mirrors are intrinsically associated with our identity today, nature hadn't foreseen anything to enable us to contemplate our own faces. There is no mirror tree. It might seem absurd, but like a child who realizes one day that her hamburger comes from the body of a slaughtered animal, I understood that evening that mirrors were a human invention. Six thousand years before our era, at the time of the Egyptians. Before that, human beings hadn't been able to see their faces clearly. It was impossible, just as it was impossible to hear one's own voice for people who lived before the invention of sound recorders. Or just as today we cannot possibly know the effect our skin has on another person when that person caresses us. Of course reflections on the surface of calm water have always provided glimpses of shapes and traits. But that reflection on clear water led Narcissus to his bitter fate. And there is no water deep enough to offer the same clarity provided by the simplest of mirrors. I put Stalin down on the floor in front of the standing mirror in the bedroom on Cimburkova Street and observed him. I quickly understood that he was totally indifferent and obviously considered the cat who suddenly appeared before him an absurdity, since it had neither smell nor personality. Stalin did not for one second recognize himself. Then I looked at myself and wondered what I could recognize about myself, and I asked myself who was right, me or Stalin? Studying my face, I saw what I saw every day, what, for reasons I'd never questioned, I called "me." Then I had the almost painful sense that my face, although clearly mine, wasn't me but a shell of skin through which I considered the world and that nothing could be more different than me and this face that represents me. I didn't recognize myself in it. I came to the realization that I undoubtedly would have been much happier, much freer at least, if I had remained unaware of my face, if it had remained unknown to me, a mystery, an enigma, and just as a show once up and running is no longer my responsibility, my face was no longer my business, or rather, more the business of others and that it was absurd to go on worrying about it. I was confined inside something whose sole window was this surface I called "my face" and instead of contemplating it, I'd do better to contemplate the world. Having reached this conclusion, I promptly decided that for one year, to the day, I would stop looking at my reflection, be it in a store window, a puddle of rainwater, or any other reflective surface. I was taking a break from my face. What look on my face? What's wrong with it? Suddenly I couldn't care less, that was settled, I'd let other people worry about it. After a few challenges, revolving mostly around shaving, I practised this prohibition with disconcerting ease. Week after week, without so much as a glance at my face, my sensation of it grew, and this sensation made me strangely happier than my previous obsession with its reality. The connection hadn't been lost, on the contrary. I simply had to wipe my forehead, or smile, or frown, take off my glasses, put them back on again, or rub my eyes and the intrinsic attachment between us was re-established. It was no longer me, but it rebecame an intimate companion, with the result that going for a year without looking at it once became easy because I'd stopped thinking about it. I no longer spoke of "my face" but of "it," "the face I live with," and this distancing from the possessive pronoun "my" is undoubtedly a precious gift. In much the same way, as of this morning regarding confinement: stop taking it personally, stop thinking that anything can be mine in this state of affairs. Things accompany us but are not us. I had developed a sixth sense for seeing mirrors ahead before I looked into them. Like Perseus approaching the Gorgon Medusa, it was important to avert my gaze, to shift my eyes in elevators, dressing rooms, restaurants, stores, and cars. And the more I stayed away from mirrors, the more I had the feeling that I was disrobing a form of alienation I had never been aware of. I was disrobing, that is to say, I was shedding my robes to face the outside, as if, from behind this face, I had found a door opening onto fresh air. I didn't become indifferent to what my face could reveal, but I found a mirror in the eyes of others. It was easy to tell what was wrong: my hair, my fatigue, my sadness, or my anger. Time went by until one winter evening in the town of Rimouski, on the banks of the Saint Lawrence, for no particular reason, I decided to put an end to this regimen and to look at myself in the mirror. I opened my eyes, raised my head, and I saw the copy of an original that had gone missing. In the same way, facing the mirror in the bathroom this morning, I understood that this confinement brought an obligation to remain riveted to this reflection, and being obliged to look at it, no matter how often I turned around or turned away, I would always end up facing myself and I was going to have to live with that. That, at any rate, was my interpretation of the injunction our politicians kept repeating yesterday on all the media: "This is only the beginning. This is only the beginning." So it's impossible to forget oneself, to turn away from this mirror. But what is this all about? What have we stolen from the gods so that like Prometheus, on a cliff exposed to violent winds, his hands and legs bound, his flanks pierced, we are now chained by unbreakable bonds to our houses? What have we usurped? And to give it to whom? Prometheus was punished for his love of humankind, but for what love are we being punished? For having offered fire to mortals, Prometheus was chained to his rock and sentenced to being the eternal prey of the eagles who, day after day, in an unending cycle, would relentlessly eviscerate him and devour his liver. And with no hope of dying, with a wound that constantly healed, a liver constantly renewed, the eagles that would return day after day, and before leaving, as they soared, they would release their immense cry, reminding Prometheus, "This is only the beginning." After leaving the bathroom, while preparing breakfast for the children, slicing apples and pears, I wondered how Prometheus's pain had evolved with time. He had been sentenced to suffer the same violence eternally but he hadn't lost his memory, so forced to face it, he, Prometheus, the generous god, had had time to get to know his pain, time to know every variation of it, perhaps to tame it and even to see it, not as something that was his, but as a companion. And from that point on, by taming it, he became his pain, it became him, and it ceased to be a torture, on the contrary. All the vicissitudes in our lives can become material for whatever we choose. So what do I choose to make of this situation? For the time being, writing. But as the days advance towards a horizon that continues to retreat, the skyline shrinks beneath my feet and, as I write, the same question often returns, obsessing and threatening me: "How can you go on speaking of poetry, go on hoping to find a single word for this journal, without being engulfed by the anaesthesia produced by this beastly everyday reality? How can you go on?" Not far from the village of Oqaatsut in Greenland, beyond the dump where the corpses of dogs are tossed in a pile, a long hike led me one day to a house where the windows revealed a room with walls lined with books and a sofa and armchairs in the middle. I knocked on the door. No answer. The door wasn't bolted. It was cold outside. I entered, driven by an irrepressible urge, despite the fear of being discovered by the owner. A wonderful silence reigned in the house. I went in, I looked at the books, I sat down on the sofa to catch my breath. And before I realized it, I dozed off and fell asleep, only to wake up incapable, for a few seconds, of knowing where I was. How long had I been there? The sun was going down and looking up, I panicked, seeing a man seated across from me, watching me. My fright was so great, I jumped up startled, and he promptly gestured to reassure me. And without saying a word, he poured a cup of coffee and passed it to me. I drank. He spoke neither French nor English. I pointed to the window and the books, I made gestures. He smiled, communicating that he understood what had happened to me. We sat there facing each other. We could only look at each other. So I studied his face, he studied mine, and we understood a bit better not only who the other man was, but who we were ourselves. Night fell. I stood up and bid him goodbye, and I left. A rush of happiness came over me in the dull glare of the glaciers. There, so far away from everything, walking in the silence of the north, poetry had appeared when I least expected it. Thinking about that now, chained like everyone else to the rock of my mirror, waiting day after day for the terrifying visit of the eagles, thinking that although poetry often remains inaccessible, it hasn't completely abandoned us, as long as we dare enter uninvited. There's no point searching for a door, or seeking to understand. Simply, one day we will be outside again.

FRIDAY, APRIL 10, DAY 25

For several years now, I've been waiting for my father's death. I've been waiting for it the way we wait for pain to end. For several years now, I've hoped for a morning when he'd fail to wake up, so he'd no longer feel the pangs of sorrow and his eyes could finally find peace. But instead, by a cruel turn of events, given our state of confinement, I now live in fear of the message, the telephone call that could announce his death. For although I've hoped for my father's death, I've always hoped he'd be spared any distress and his distress would be immense, I know, if he were to die with no one at his bedside, with no one to hold his hand. That would send him to his death convinced that up until his last breath, he was cursed by the gods, since circumstances, often violent, will have forced him more often than not throughout his life to live alone, far from his loved ones. Born in 1928 in the Chouf mountain region of Lebanon, the sole survivor among his siblings, he finds himself living today, at age ninety-two, in one room in a retirement home in Montréal. For my father, like many people his age around the world, confinement in a retirement home where visitors are forbidden can feel like a double jail sentence. For many of these elderly people, visitors are the sole joy in their long days, and more than just a joy, visitors are the cornerstone of their psyche. Old age and the accompanying illnesses and the shadow of death can bring a great loss of self-esteem if, in addition to the challenges of aging, they feel abandoned. Old or young, we all have a sharp awareness of our personal integrity and our dignity. Visits from loved ones help the elderly in retirement homes to keep their precious sense of dignity alive, and for my father, whose two sons live far away, in one case five thousand kilometres to the east and in the other case four thousand kilometres to the west, the sum of his loved ones, his friends, family members, and acquaintances resides in the sixty-year-old person of his only daughter, who ever since he was placed in this home has never failed to visit him every day after work. "Where is she now?" he must wonder when his spirits flag. "Where is she?" Until it became impossible because of the lockdown, not a day passed without her bringing him some of the dishes he loves, without her taking the time to chat with him, showing him photos of the blessed years in Lebanon before the war, when he still owned his 1957 Chevrolet, when he still had what he called a "position that inspired respect." Not a single day without her playing a card game with him, asking him questions, showing an interest in him, and kissing him goodbye before going home. Among the most beautiful images in literature, those that feature the bond between father and daughter are often the most moving: King Lear and Cordelia, Oedipus and Antigone, and if I may, I would add to this pantheon of love my father and my sister. When, after years of wandering, he had nowhere else to go, he lived in her home for twenty-five years and she, with her inimitable grace, made him feel as if she was the one living in his. What I'm saying about my father can certainly be said about all the elderly living in retirement homes. Is it because I feel in my own flesh my sister's immense heart and the immense pain of my father whose existence was constantly crushed by war and exile and solitude, and who with the powerful approach of a death, stripped and cleansed by it, has become as touching as a child – is it because of all this that I cannot bear the increasingly common calculation that brutally opposes economic realism and human sacrifice? I wish my father would die, but I don't wish this death for him. I don't want to see him become a statistic, nor do I want him to be sacrificed on the altar of some GDP. Yet, day after day, the body of any old person suffering from this virus is mutating, transforming from a human body into the body politic because we seem to be irreversibly headed for the nightmare which will entail choosing, lockdown or not, between the young and the old, between the economy and the lives of the most vulnerable – choosing who must be sacrificed. For a sacrifice must take place, a horrendous choice if no cure is found. And in no way is a pangolin or a bat responsible for our nightmares. We are the architects of a terrifying labyrinth whose mysterious ways have become inextricably entangled over the past thirty years, leading to the tragic trap we have set ourselves. How to solve the equation humanity is facing? *King Lear* ends on a note of reconciliation in Edgar's sublime lines: "The weight of this sad time we must obey; / Speak what we feel, not what we ought to say. / The oldest hath borne most; we that are young / Shall never see so much, nor live so long." Followed by the last stage direction: "Exeunt, with a dead march." That stage direction is devastating because it's impossible for us today. What actions can we invent together to achieve such a dignified end: leaving with the body to the sound of a death march ...? Dignity is what matters dearly to our elderly. My father, like so many others, doesn't fear confinement as much as he fears solitude at the moment of his death. War, it's true, had accustomed my father to solitude. For years on end, having stayed in Lebanon to continue working while we were in Paris, then in Montréal, he had to learn to cope with unhappiness. For years, much later when I would stop by to visit him, I often asked him about those terrible years. He always avoided the question, finding clever ways to change the subject and bring me back to the question of money, his favourite subject. But as the years went by, with the onset of old age, illness, and the prospect of death, his heart opened and he began to speak more openly, freed from the sclerosis of shame that had restrained him for such a long time. "How did you manage on your own during the war, Papa? When the bombing was so intense, not only was it impossible to leave the house but it was impossible to communicate with us or with anyone? Internet didn't exist, cellphones didn't exist, and the phone lines were always down. So what did you do? I've never seen you reading a book, and there was no television. Nothing. How did you spend your time, when during the worst periods of bombing, you were forced to stay home alone for weeks on end? How did you manage?" I think I asked him that question every Sunday for ten years. And one day, instead of dismissing the question with his usual answer, "I don't know. What do you expect me to say?! That's how it was, there was no way around it. What do you think we could do? I don't know. How can you expect me to remember? Stop asking me these questions, *yallah khalas*!" ... One day, instead, he started to laugh and he said: "You won't believe it, but I'll tell you anyway, and you can use it for one of your plays and you'll stop thinking your father's an idiot and it will be a great comedy. Your plays are always too sad. How much do you earn with every play you write?"

"Papa, don't change the subject, you said I wouldn't believe you. So, what did you do during the war when you couldn't leave the house? What did you do?!"

"What do you think I did?"

"That's what I'm asking you: What did you do?"

For a moment I thought it was a lost cause and that we would end up arguing again, like every time he was about to talk about something that took him back to that humiliating period of his life when, because of the war, he lost everything he had and was no longer able to feed his family and he was forced to ask his children to find work. "Don't worry, I'll leave you something," he'd tell us again and again, and the more he said it, the less he had to leave to anyone. And to no avail, we'd tell him, we'd try to reassure him that he didn't realize he had already given us the essential: his extreme sensitivity and his imaginative mind he was unaware of himself.

"Tell me, Papa, what did you do all by yourself?"

"Why do you want to know?"

"Because you never tell me anything. And I want to stop

asking myself these questions. Can't you understand, I'm sick of wondering why we left Lebanon, who was shooting at who during that war, what was the war about, why is my mother buried in Montréal, and why don't I speak Arabic anymore? So you should consider yourself lucky that I'm sparing you these difficult questions, you hear me, I'm just asking you one simple question, one friendly question: How did you spend your time during the bombings? Why don't you dare answer me? What's the deal? Did you hire women, did you hold parties, did you smoke weed, or all that at the same time? What did you do? Tell me! Nothing would shock me, nothing would offend me. Except your silence! Tell me!"

"Well ... spiritism."

"Pardon me?"

"I practised spiritism. I called upon spirits. I was alone, I didn't want to be alone, but I was alone. You can't imagine what it's like to feel your life slip through your fingers and have no one to talk to. Daytime or nighttime didn't matter anymore. I slept when sleep came, then I'd go around in circles until I fell asleep again. You, you have your theatre, you have your friends, you have your family, so you have no idea. One night, I sat down at my table ... you remember the little table where we used to have breakfast, the round red table ... I set out the letters of the alphabet and I called, asking if a spirit was there ... First my mother's spirit came. Then my father's. Then the spirits of those long dead, those who worked the land in the mountains before me, your ancestors who, up until me, were all illiterate and who suffered hardships long forgotten today, back when we were under the yoke of the Ottomans. And night after night, day after day, I spent my time with them. There was no more war, no more worries. We had long conversations together, and that's all I did. Nothing else existed. I forgot everything else. Everything. Until I felt overwhelmed by how much I missed you, my children. For the first time, I felt the desire for affection, the need to hold you in my arms. I couldn't bear being away from you, I felt how much I loved you and I started to call on you."

"What do you mean?"

"You heard me. I missed you, so I called your spirits. What did you expect me to do? If it worked with the dead, it could work with the living. So I tried, and it worked. I called your mother's spirit, your sister's spirit, your brother's spirit, and yours. And I'd spend time with each of you like that, we'd chat, we were together and during those moments, locked up, alone, I was painfully aware of how nothing is more beautiful than being together. But we weren't together. So you asked me what I did, that's what I did."

I remained speechless. It was snowing that day in Montréal. And last night, remembering all that, thinking about the pain and the light that travel through every human heart, I became aware of the storms that live in my father's soul. I wished I could go see him today, but of course I can't. No planes, no way. Even if I went on foot, if I crossed the Bering Strait and walked through Alaska and across Canada from west to east, all the way to Montréal, I wouldn't be allowed to enter the institution where he lives because of the lockdown regulations.

So tonight it was my turn to clear my table and place the letters of the alphabet in a circle. I turned off the light and I called upon my father's spirit. I spoke the words of a son to him, I spoke about the powerful bond, I told him I would remain the guardian of our memories and I would find the words to express our troubles. And even if, in another life, we might have been closer to each other, we should have no regrets. Everything is a gift.

MONDAY, APRIL 13, DAY 28

The scene takes place in 1986, around the kitchen table in a small apartment in an unspeakably ugly building located at 360 boulevard Thompson in Montréal. My mother is stripping the leaves off three bunches of parsley, and my brother is filling both sides of every page of his notebook with factorials, square roots, sums, equations and inequations, juggling infinites, sines and cosines, grunting and sighing as my mother looks on, increasingly exasperated. Erasures, new attempts, more erasures, crumpled sheets of paper, frowns, logarithms, algorithms for a whole hour. Witnessing what seems like a losing battle, seeing her son close to passing out, my mother, unable to contain herself, in the typically Mediterranean tone of voice that leaves no room for negotiation, asks him why he's sighing like that, it's driving her crazy, and what in heaven's blessed name is he fussing over for the past two hours! All that in Arabic, which is the language best suited for someone who wants to express her frustrations, complaints, and lamentations. And my brother, carrying on, without even raising his head, without realizing it, replies: "I am trying to prove that one is different from zero." Bewilderment in the kitchen. My mother, and this is very rare, falls silent, dumbstruck, her mouth open, her eyes bulging, a parsley stem in her hands. Then, gathering her wits, unable to watch her son suffer any longer without coming to his rescue, leans towards him and announces with maternal certainty: "They're different, my son, believe me, it's different." My brother looks up and breaks out laughing, and, without a moment's hesitation, writes in his notebook, "One is different from zero," and below that, as fundamental proof of his solution, he writes, "My mother said so. QED." This little anecdote came to mind a while ago, remembering that, among a thousand other things I owe him, it's my brother who made me understand that what seems most obvious to us is always the most difficult to prove. And this hypothesis, to use his vocabulary, became a game between us when, needing to break the boredom of an interminable wait, in the car, on the bus, on foot, or at some government office for the insignificant renewal of some equally insignificant paper, one would challenge the other to demonstrate the proof of a seemingly obvious statement.

"Prove to me that you exist," my brother challenges me one day.

"Easy," I answer, "I exist because I know I do."

"That doesn't prove a thing! When you're dreaming, sometimes you're sure you're not dreaming, but you are. Same thing now, but without the negation. You think you exist, but you don't. You are only dreaming."

"Okay," I answer, "but if I were dreaming, I'd wake up, but I am not waking up, therefore, I'm not dreaming."

"Therefore, nothing! Maybe you're just a life that almost existed and which consists only of reminiscences, and right now, this life you think is a dream is an existence that never took place."

"Hmm, okay, but you see me here, since you're talking to me, therefore, if you see me, I exist!"

"No. Maybe I am just one of the characters imagined in your illusion and it's you making me talk."

"Okay, but if I'm making you talk, I must exist."

"No, because maybe you are hallucinating!"

"Fine then, exactly, if I am hallucinating, it means I am not 'nothing,' since 'nothing' cannot hallucinate, and if I am not nothing, it means I am something: therefore, I exist."

And we could go on like that until nightfall, until I fell asleep without having demonstrated, in my brother's eyes, the proof of my existence. Very much like this morning. Looking outside, waiting, while keeping the required distance, for the arrival of masked bunnies and their delivery of Easter eggs we will not be allowed to touch for several hours, ensuring that any possible fragments of coronavirus that might have stuck to the wrapping have had time to die and dry up like lizards rotting in the sun, my six-and-a-half-year-old son tells me that he might already be grown up, and that maybe today, in this moment, he is simply the memory of himself. That is the sentence that took me back to my brother, making me think: "Oh, no! No, no, no, no, no, no! Here we go! Here we go again! That stupid game is starting over. Now you have one hour, you must all prove that one is different from zero."

"What do you mean?" I ask him.

"Well, maybe I am only my own memory, and right now I am grown up and I am remembering myself."

He was on the verge of tears. How can this kind of abstraction come from the mind of a little boy? Leaning over to his height, staring at him, I had the feeling I was looking at a painting by Pierre Soulages, whose deeply luminous black strokes had suddenly taken shape in the depth of the eyes of this six-and-a-half-year-old little boy who was looking outside, waiting for the bunnies to arrive. How to prove to him that the present was real? How to prove to him that life wasn't elsewhere, that he wasn't elsewhere? We started hunting for eggs and we found them one after the other, with their colourful aluminum wrappers that we would use later to make metallic costumes for Playmobil heroes. Afterwards, we set ourselves up at the kitchen table, colouring sheet after sheet of paper, on both sides, in blue, black, yellow, red, green, pink, for thousands of snails, each with its own shell, its own colour, before playing cards and reading comics. At four o'clock we ate the chocolates, then we made origami fish, and all the while I could sense his quivering worry, as if this lockdown, having blurred the divisions of time – yesterday, today, tomorrow – was telescoping different periods, past and future, with the result that in his mind an existence that hadn't yet taken place created an uncertainty and triggered a fear in this little philosopher that he had never felt before. "I miss my friends," he told me. "I want to go back to school. I want to be after, I want today to be a memory." Talking with him about this after, talking with him about time passing and his perception of his own life, I could see a thought take shape in him, a new way of handling abstraction which endowed him with a seriousness that he didn't have before the lockdown, or, rather, that had not yet revealed itself. We are secret chambers and it only takes one event for light, shifting with the impact of shock, to reveal an angle which, until that moment, had always been buried in total darkness. And traumas do not always arrive with a thundering noise. For the past month spent like this, no bomb came to destroy our street, no sound of machine-gun fire, no explosions, no snipers, nothing. We have running water, electricity, we have the internet. Today's landscapes resemble those of yesterday. But we are living with a shock that is traumatizing us in homeopathic doses. I held him in my arms.

"If you are the memory of yourself later," I asked him, "and in reality, in this moment, you are a man remembering yourself as a child, does the idea of already being a man make you happy or make you feel worried?"

"It makes me worried and it makes me happy."

"What worries you?"

"That we won't be together anymore."

"And what makes you happy?"

"Well, if I'm grown up, that means I'm with my friends. When I'm grown up, I always want to be with my friends. Except if there's still the virus. Then I'll have to be in confinement."

At six and a half, I thought, I wasn't capable of saying the words "in confinement."

"Yes, but there won't still be the virus," I said.

"You can't be sure."

Those few, distressingly true words, "You can't be sure," were enough to make me stop talking, make me understand that beyond the confinement, beyond the huge effort we were making to make their days enjoyable, to explain as casually as possible the political and public-health decisions that dictate our daily lives, that despite our affection, despite the films projected on walls, despite the crêpes, the waffles, the tarts, the games, the activities, the Skype calls with their friends, their grandparents, despite the thousands of litres of normalcy we tried to inject into this situation, despite the love, the tenderness, despite all that, pungent worry and fear were steeping in the children's minds, like cheap tea steeping for too long in boiling water. We will have to rebuild many things after. And it will take a long time. But most of all, there will be many things to be deconstructed and that might take even longer. Nothing succeeded in deconstructing the architecture that war erected in me. How to deconstruct, stone by stone, the structures of memory? How to prove that one is different from zero? How to deconstruct fear in the hearts of children? I went to his bedside to say goodnight. I turned off the main light, leaving only the night light, I lay down beside him, and I told him I could hardly wait for the time when the man he would become would spontaneously call his father and suggest that they eat together. We will spend the evening together, talking about all sorts of things, we will drink wine and make jokes, before leaving, him to join his friends and me to go home.

"You will be an old grampa, I'll have to drive you home in my flying car."

"Yes, I'll be a very old grampa."

His drawings were scattered over my work table, but strangely, carried away by the mood, my thoughts were more with the man I had imagined than with the child I had just put to bed, and I had an overwhelming desire, maybe as a way of deconfining myself, to speak to him. So I began to write to one while thinking of the other.

My dear little boy,

Writing these four words to you is so emotional for me. They render the man you are so real in this today that is yours, when in this day that is mine, you are still just a child. So I am writing this letter to the man that you have not yet become for me, yet the man you have become, since there you are reading it. You will have found it, I suppose, by accident, on the USB key where I keep the secrets of your childhood. I don't know how old you are, I don't know what the world has become, I don't even know if these keys still work, but I hope that, discovering it, remembering your father, you will manage to open it. And through the magic of writing, this letter will become the thin wall that connects us, and between the today where I am writing to you – where you are beginning to decipher sentences, where you are afraid of the dark, where you believe in magic – and the day when you will read this, each word of my letter lives in the present; and if, for example, in the moment where I write "I love you," years later, there you are, reading "I love you." And what more can I write to you than "I love you" while we are going through what we are going through in these weeks of confinement of which you might have only a vague memory? What could be expressed more urgently than love? During these strange times where an invisible death is on the prowl, where the world is headed towards its ravine, a ravine that seems to be the inheritance of your generation, a father, not unreasonably, fears for his son. You draw a snail. You raise your head and smile at me. "What's the matter, Papa?" "Nothing, my son." I can't save the world. But while I fail to save it, I can at least teach you not to fear. Help you not to hesitate on the day when you will have to choose between being courageous and buying a washing machine. Most of all, teach you why you must never pronounce the words of Cain and that, whatever the price, you must remain your brother's keeper, at the risk of losing everything. I don't know where you will be reading my letter, in what time, wartime or peacetime, human time or machine time, I simply hope that your present is better than mine. We have buried ourselves alive and we have deprived ourselves of all the acts of bliss: kissing, embracing, sharing, and not one of us can dry the tears of a friend. But should your time be worse than the time of your childhood, if in the moment when you are reading my letter, you are in turn living in fear, I would like to think this letter will give you a bit of the courage I sometimes failed to have, and that, thinking of the things we often talked about together, you will remember that kindness is the standard in this world, for kindness is courageous, kindness is generous, and it will never consent to be like an ambush which, attacking from behind, lives off the blood of others. No one can explain the greatness of those who give this world meaning. Leave courage in your wake and never accept anything that revolts you. As for me, I love you. Your father loves you. Know that and never doubt it.

TUESDAY, APRIL 14, DAY 29

This evening, at 8:02 p.m., the president of the République spoke to the nation. As befitted his position, he used the level of language the gravity of the situation required of him. I will now provide a translation for those who wish to hear the clearings and the forests. However, I must warn the purists. The rules of translation will not be respected, or to be more precise, my ambition is to surpass those rules, to take the text and bring it to a boil, to press it with the branding iron of writing. You are about to read a giant betrayal of the original text in that, taking the presidential speech by surprise, I will attempt to stage a coup of the poetic State. How to appropriate language other than through the use of the narrative "I"? That is, using the "I" of the child as well as the "I" of the writer, the personal pronoun that dares, with no pretension, nor desire to offend, take possession of all the words in all languages, boldly, without asking permission or paying royalties. Fair warning having been given; here is the translation of the text for those who are interested.

For each and every one of you this evening, my words will be a shard of our pain, but also of our barbarity. We are how we are, but for the most part we cannot know the hour of our death. In my case, every evening I approach the ravine of my table and I let myself tumble into words. I fall every night, mystified by how long this fall takes, and I remember those bodies in free fall, little commas falling from the Twin Towers in New York, an image that will undoubtedly remain the matrix of this century we are navigating, the twenty-first century of our era, now emerging from its adolescence. Remember. Those human commas, tumbling in the sky of New York, many of us, petrified, saw them on our screens, commas, semicolons, then the full stops in a series of horrors, from the trenches of 1914 to the machetes of Rwanda, all that shattering with a dull thud on the pavement in New York. It was the end of a century. We thought we had reached the end of History, we never could have imagined that we had simply reached the beginning. And since then, always on the shores of foreign seas, when we look up at an exquisitely blue sky, those commas will float in the gaze of many of us, slicing our eyes more purely than the razor in Buñuel's Un chien andalou. *Who hasn't imagined at some point that they were in one of those towers, office worker or secretary, preferring to jump rather than endure the suffering and despair of that moment of suffocation when the fire and the dust, filling their lungs, prevent them from breathing? Who wouldn't prefer to escape that hell in the grace of a vertiginous fall of hundreds of metres during which, a bird for a fraction of a second, the lungs reclaim breath, air, relief. Who hasn't imagined being the comma in the place of the comma floating in the void of the fall? This thought has come over me, for one, and my mind always panics. In contemporary history, there was clearly a before and an after September 11, just as there was a before and an after the* Charlie Hebdo *shooting, a before the November 13 and an after the November 13 attack, just as today, we decree with the same conviction that there will be a before COVID-19 and an after COVID-19. All of these befores and afters are true, not one is a lie, that is why, dear compatriots, it will be said of our era that it was the tragic era of macabre parentheses which, opening, closing, before and after, never stopped blocking the light. I am aware of the extent to which we are creatures of sensation, creatures of sensitivities, but we have forgotten that. Because a position of power brings its share of brutalities, I, for one, have also forgotten that, at the core of each of us, there is a secret parchment called fragility. It's that fragility that has caught up with us all today. Me, first and foremost. It is what this pandemic forces us to bring to the surface of our consciousness and orders us to consider a top priority. I will watch over it personally. We are in exile. Although we are in our homes, this pandemic has thrown us out on the roads of exile, an exile that has no name but it remains an exile. I have taken the time to listen to the women and men who have encountered hardships on those roads, I went to see them myself, personally, to better understand, to hear and to listen, and they all, each in their own language, some coming from the north, many from the south, made me understand, despite what various philosophers wanted us to believe, that exile is never a situation, but rather thwarted action: to walk in place, to stop without finding shelter, to catch one's breath without finding air. So this thwarting will continue. On the long spit of sand stretching out before us, if the footsteps we will leave manage to capture the elegance of our limping march, then something powerful will emerge, and we will have been right, truly, to invest the battle with our capacity for laughter, companionship, and love.*

What I have to say to you this evening is inaudible to everyone, what I must say to you is unbearable for everyone. Yet I will say it. In short: From a microscopic point of view, there is basically no difference between happiness and unhappiness, just as it is impossible to say which slope owns the crest of the mountain. What remains is the possibility of choice; and it is always possible to change our minds and decide that the crest will always belong to the sunny side. Perhaps also because power implies the art of making mistakes while always being right, the art of failing in order always to succeed.

Giving this speech tonight feels like an invisible shift in an attempt at revolution. I would like to invite you all to join this revolution. Speaking and storming the Bastille are different in that taking the Bastille requires labourers, masons, plasterers who know where to strike to bring down a wall, while taking the floor requires the edification of letters in a speech capable of igniting the sparks that will reveal a horizon for us.

My dear compatriots, in my desire to speak of the weeks to come, I shared with you the hope I place in sensitivity, I evoked fragility, and without trembling I spoke candidly of the exile that is currently our lot. I did so in my own way and I realize that my language doesn't become my age or my standing, but it is our behaviour over the past decades and our betrayal of what is dearest that force me to speak to you as I am. At least rest assured that the brutality of my words translates the transparency of my intentions. I will always tell it as it is. That is why I must introduce two words which will appear even more unacceptable than those that came before, even more unbearable, but I dare utter them here, since, despite everything, I am confident that you will hear them for what they're worth, because as tiresome as they might sound, these two words are what gives us a reason to live and to act! And especially because these two words will be present in the last hour of the last day of everyone, not as attending doctors, not as friends or relatives, but as the deep intuitions of what weaves the life of every human being, words that bear witness to our existence. Those two words are: art and tragedy.

Remember. The Egyptians of antiquity, believing in life after this life, embalmed their pharaohs to lead them to their dark residence. In their stone graves, weapons and food were placed at their bedside in anticipation of their awakening, and often, when the deceased was a great monarch, in addition to food, the best soldiers were sent to the depths of the earth with the dead to ensure their protection and to serve them in the afterlife. At the death of their pharaohs, the Egyptians of antiquity sent their most valiant soldiers to their graves, and no doubt they felt great sorrow, for while the life of the living must be preserved, there must also be consolation for the dead. To settle this conflict between life and death, certain silent spirits, wise and wild, certain scribes had the strange idea of sending into the tomb, as protection for the pharaoh, in place of the warriors themselves, their statuary replicas. The Egyptians proceeded to create the most beautiful paintings, the most beautiful statues possible. One for each warrior. And for the first and undoubtedly the last time in the history of humanity, works of art saved human lives by going in their place into the cold depths of the stone graves. What did these men see, when at the sealing of the grave, they watched the works representing them being buried in their place? And what has that way of seeing become today? Who is capable of projecting it beyond themselves? Well, dear compatriots, that way of seeing is what will save us from the pandemic today; these images, protectors of our fears, will show us the way. For all too long, we have insisted upon stripping death of its mysteries, and we believed we succeeded. That is why I have decided that all the elderly who die from now on will have the right, despite exile, to the imprint of the mystery of the people they loved and who are dear to them. What are we waiting for? In the accumulation of information and wealth, what are we waiting for? In the blind passing of time, in the multiplying of organizations and reorganizations and the weight of information, what are we waiting for? When the gods themselves, throwing themselves into the blaze of their disappearance, committing suicide one after the other, each performing self-massacre, one hanging himself, another slitting her veins, and yet another drowning himself in the river of human tears, in this suicide of the gods that has left a void for so long, what are we waiting for? What can we still expect? What can we still hope for if not the attempt to care for everyone, from the first to the last? These questions, all these questions, I know they have something to do with the visions of the warriors who watched works of art being buried in their place so that they need not leave behind sunlight and the blueness of the sky. It might not make sense, but one work of art for each one of us is our last chance. Humanity has forever oscillated between art and tragedy. We forget what we have been through, and words are always there to recreate memory. That is why, dear compatriots, forgetting is the tragedy while art is its indecipherable memory. One couldn't exist without the other.

How I would have loved to announce to you tonight that a work of art will replace me to address you. But in all honesty, I must tell you, our era is not yet capable of facing such naivety. Too much suffering, too much pain, too much injustice for which we are all responsible. Me, first and foremost.

*To address you, I must tune into your pain. For you,
in turn, to persist in innocence would be its own
form of insult and injury. It would lead to the death
of thousands of people. We have no choice but to
engage with the infection. Step into it. At the same
time, on the crest of the mountain, between the slope
of loss and that of joy, we can always choose joy. And
I call this choice tragic. In the unbridled schizophrenia
of feeling torn, as if distracted, distraught, I chose to
constantly proceed hand in hand in the clandestine
position of the child who, under the table, hidden by
the overhanging tablecloth, seeing the game of the
adults' legs, understands in advance their bitter sadness and their death to come. For what is a president
of the République other than that child under the
table reinventing a world to come, still imperceptible
to the adults who are there in the thrall of the present?*

*For seventy-five years now, we can no longer be sure
of ourselves. Constantly forced to feel our way. How
could this not be the case since men burned men, with
no other reason than the desire to burn the Book of
which they are the people? And no prophet to divide
the waters and come to their rescue, no beauty to die
in their place. That happened and it is like a bridge
that collapsed on the road of our return. We can't
get back to before the obliteration, where even the
letters of the alphabet burned. To make words today,
we have nothing but ashes. So we make words with
our memory of the letters; now writing is an act of
remembering itself, always. That is why children
absolutely must rediscover the pathways of terror.
How else can we teach them that writing an A is no
longer writing an A, but rather writing an A that
can only remember what the A once was, before the*

abyss, long ago? That is what I am asking of you, despite the immense effort you will all have to make.

It will be like the creation of a new show. Something of the theatres will have to remain definitively closed so that artists can once again learn the art of breaking and entering. Too much complicity, for too long now, has been woven into the relationship between art and power, between the men in power and the artists, too many connections, too much seduction. I expect artists to practise insubordination, since what organization can tolerate breaking and entering? The state demands explanations, it can't accept insubordination and requires that permission be asked for everything. Everything that artists have the duty to refuse, even when the state uses all its powers to force them to submit. The role of art is always to escape in order to invent a new language incomprehensible to the very state that wants to make it obey.

Now it is time for me to speak to you about the after. As you know, there's been much talk about new computer technology. Technology that provides access to countless activities: reading the newspapers and books, watching films, organizing time and materials, playing games. But at rush hour in the Métro, where strangers face each other, forced to look into each other's eyes, forced, in such close quarters, to stare at hands holding poles, the virus is spreading, since there is no way of knowing what others are experiencing. I can try with all my might and sensitivity to focus on the mole between the two fingers of the hand holding on, at my eye level, to the pole in the Métro car so as not to fall, I will never know if the person there is grappling with a tragedy or not. I will never know what she is going through. I can't tell, looking with all the empathy I can muster at the twenty-odd people standing with me at the bakery, who lived through the war, who cannot have children, who is in deep mourning. We are walking mysteries to each other and now we only see each other as threats. That is why I have asked the mayors and regional administrators to ensure that every woman and man, especially in public transportation, be provided with a book of poetry. Not to fulfill a cultural duty, but to heal. Indeed we believe that of all the artists, in order to write, poets must connect with that particle of tragedy within themselves which would be fatal in large quantities, but distilled in a poem protects anyone who reads it from necrosis of the soul, for a poem acts like a vaccine against the virus of despair. All the industries in our country have been mobilized to make a poem available to every French citizen, to everyone who desires it. Because, dear compatriots, we are buildings inhabited by tenants we know nothing about. Our well-maintained façades look fine. But inside, who is the mad insomniac who paces round in circles for hours turning the lights on and off? These tenants who inhabit us accumulate memories and objects. They collect, weigh themselves down. The totalitarianism of goods quickly purchased, quickly assembled and used, quickly discarded on the sidewalks, quickly burned. The refuse site of urban cities. Yes. We are buildings with countless rooms, countless hallways, dark corridors leading to staircases that go up and down. There are myriad labyrinths accessible by elevator, leading to basements, entire unsuspected worlds, full of anger, sensuality, sexuality, fluidity, stupor, stammering. There are many chimneys that haven't been swept for ages, many secret passages, liquid, organic rooms, there, in the dark buildings we are, there are aquarium rooms where the strangest,

*most carnivorous, most terrifying fish swim! Interior
gardens where wild animals roam freely, magnificent
beasts: pumas, lions, cheetahs, crocodiles, and sabre-
tooth tigers. Myriad birds inhabit the space, nesting
in the antique candelabras, the doorways, and cor-
nices. But all of that, that splendid world, remains
unexplored, unknown. The tenants who live there,
in the buildings we are, are terrified by the prospect
of leaving the room where they are confined: domestic
world where the heating is pleasant, lovely tea room
protected from pain, small reassuring interior that is
becoming smaller without warning, since the less we
hurt, the less we want to hurt, and the less we tolerate
hurting, the more things will hurt us. Without the
experience of being our own pain, impossible to tolerate pain, impossible, therefore, to expand the world.
Impossible to open the door. For where is the key
capable of opening that service entrance to allow the
tenants to explore their wildlife? That, my compatriots, will be the challenge of deconfinement.*

*That is why, today more than ever, poet rhymes with
pyromaniac. For what happens when a building is
ravaged by fire? The windows shatter, the inhabitants open their doors and start running around! The
extinguishers are triggered, flooding all the previous
comfort, breaking everything, destroying everything.
Well that is the revolution I invite you to join. Art as
the act of a warrior who wages a battle of which I
am at once the terrain, the enemy, the weapon, and
the fighter. That is the reality of the virus. Go to war
for an inner war. To be at war to free the vultures and
hyenas prepared to devour the carrion that thinks it's
alive inside me. The convenience of my convenient
situation, living in retreat, thanks to the blood of
others. That is the virus.*

Commotion: that is the vaccine we are seeking with all our might!
Dear compatriots, tonight, no "welcome,"no "thank you,"
no hugs, nothing, I mean, nothing,
so as to preserve, powerful and vibrant, the desire to rediscover
words, words as actions, actions as life, beautiful and wise and
wild life.
Dear compatriots, take care of yourselves.
Long live tragedy, long live poetry.

WEDNESDAY, APRIL 15, DAY 30

I sat down on the curb of the sidewalk. Across the street, an old stone wall encloses the superb garden at the Maison nationale des artistes. Subtly disorganized in the tradition of an English garden, this space is all the more romantic because it is not open to the public and this prohibition awakens the most fabulous fantasies in me. From the street, we can see tall, majestic trees. Many ash trees, many sycamores, pines, beech and linden trees. One day the caretaker, with whom I was chatting, told me about trees that grow in part of the garden invisible from the street: a thorny locust, a weeping ash, a Japanese pagoda tree, and a Judas tree. "A vegetal compatriot," I thought, and now, in Nogent-sur-Marne, I feel less alone. Last year there was one exceptional day where we were allowed to enter the garden for a few hours. I went up to the open gate and at the last minute, I did an about-face. We all need one beauty that remains forbidden to us. A face, a perspective, a landscape, a garden. Not everything can be acquired in a straight line. In the central nave of Chartres cathedral, traced in the pavement centuries ago, there is a labyrinth 12.89 metres in diameter, which has the unique feature of being unicursal, in other words, there are no cross-roads or dead ends. It is a continuous line, curled up upon itself like a big sleeping boa whose length, if it were to unwind, would measure 261.55 metres. Anyone who enters follows a path that, beginning on the outside, will lead to the centre in a series of turns, loops, and concentric circles. Step by step, following this drawn path, the walker embarks on an inner voyage leading to the centre that constantly escapes her because one hairpin turn after another will lead away, farther away, before an opposing curve brings her closer again, and after thirty minutes of a rambling made of multiple twists and a thousand detours, she finally reaches her goal with the feeling of having walked the winding paths of her soul. Altogether, this stupefyingly symmetrical labyrinth is made up of 276 stones, a number that corresponds to the average number of days necessary for the gestation of a human being in the mother's womb. The labyrinth is a place of birth, a path where you must carry your own confusion, carry your bewilderment, and lose yourself on this trying path until you reach the centre where perhaps the word, the phrase, the words, the gestures you had been seeking all along will emerge. So I am still sitting on the curbstone, distracted from my thoughts by a robin's song. I forget Chartres and the memory of the labyrinth and I listen to the robin. He's no stranger to me, since his nest is right there, and every evening his mocking calls can be heard, just as later on, when I finish writing this text, this unicursal text whose throughline I stubbornly follow in all its loops and detours, I will hear him sing again as he has every day of this lockdown, around four o'clock in the morning. I recognize his mocking song, I recognize his winding song, always composed of inflections, loops, and detours. I'll record it in a while, if I haven't collapsed with fatigue before then. Because the fatigue increases the more I do nothing. The more I go round in circles, waiting for the hours and the days to pass. The more I look for words and let them pass, go outside for some fresh air, come to sit here on the curbstone and wait for the robin's song. And the robin sings. He will sing for a good half-hour until, just before sundown, he will fall silent. Because he will fall silent. He will have reached the goal in his labyrinth. What about us? What labyrinth are we in? When will we reach the goal? Obviously, our labyrinth is not like the one in Chartres cathedral, it is not unicursal, nor is it bicursal like the one Daedalus created according to legend to hide the Minotaur. No. Ours is acursal. In other words, no curves, no line, nothing except an atonal, white, round chamber, with no corners, no snags. We have completed the tour and we don't know where the tour began. It's like a spinning mirror, a mirror made of a thousand illusions, a thousand disillusions. And every exit we think we spot turns out to be a mirage, and day after day other labyrinths slip into it, and each one gives birth to yet another. A pandemic of labyrinths that fragments us, separates us, categorizes us. In just one month, we have become obsessed with what is collapsing in our lives and when we finally leave our homes, we risk confining ourselves more than ever in the inextricable labyrinths of our difficulties, our catastrophes, to each his own ruins, living with the feeling that we have no one who understands us, and that among the misunderstood, we are the most misunderstood of all. And sitting there on my sidewalk, the sun about to disappear behind the line of the houses and the robin about to fall silent, I stood up to watch the treetops light up in the last rays. Suddenly everything had the transparency of amber and the extravagant beauty of the light was suddenly revealed. I leaned against the wall and the stones, still warm, held me in their arms as if I'd been embraced by a statue. I let myself be rocked in the scent of the ivy. It's true, I had a deep need for affection. I longed for a kind of secret consolation, invisible to passersby who, glancing at me, would only see a vaguely pensive guy leaning on a wall. A few words were enough yesterday, during the president of the République's address, to make me understand that we will have to go without theatre for a long time. How can that not be the case? How? During the civil war, we got used to living with the war, and living with the war meant going to school with the war, going to the beach with the war, going grocery shopping with the war, and all that as long as the periods of ceasefire agreed upon by the militias lasted, then returning to the shelters when the bombing resumed, sometimes for weeks at a time. Everything stopped then, school, transportation, life, work. There was nothing to do except wait for the bombs to stop. And from ceasefire to bombing, from bombing to ceasefire, the Lebanese learned to integrate this oscillation for nineteen years. Nineteen years. We have been confined for two months and we will oscillate for approximately another year. And from confinement to deconfinement, we will go on until the cure is found. We will also learn to live with the virus. Going to school with the virus, going to work with the virus, going grocery shopping with the virus, going for a walk with the virus. I'm thinking about Theo Angelopoulos's film *Ulysses' Gaze*, I'm thinking of the last scenes in that film when fog descends on the city of Sarajevo in the middle of the civil war. The fog spreads, swells, increases, and envelopes the city's mysteries, and the camera, accompanied by the sublime music of Eleni Karaindrou, lets us see the city's ruins take on an unbearable poetic depth, as unbearable as barbaric scenes can be when they don the traits and accents of poetry. And in those streets, now invisible to the snipers, the population takes advantage of this protective curtain and emerges from the shelters and resumes the conviviality of life. One scene shows a theatre troupe performing for a few spectators in the middle of the street. It only lasts for the span of the fog, then everything begins again, the noise of the bombs and machine guns, and everyone scurries back to their shelters. I'm thinking about that. As evening falls I am also thinking about the inaccessible garden I see across from me, I think about that Judas tree. I know it's there, but I also know that it's prohibited for me. Thinking of that prohibition, a sudden metallic emotion pierces my throat with its unspeakably violent blade. That's when I understand. Truly understand. I understand in my flesh that we probably have to prepare for a long separation. The oscillation between confinement and deconfinement doesn't suit theatre. What I love most in the world risks falling silent. Risks becoming prohibited. Unless a saving fog falls over us, a fog that will permit clandestine gatherings, a fog that will prompt us to reinvent a way of carrying on. The power of theatre resides in its craft. It has survived crises, it has survived wars, it has survived dictatorships, it has survived all sorts of brutalities. We will simply have to enter with no hope of a straight line, but, on the contrary, follow the curves, the loops, the detours, the circles and sinuosities to reach the goal. Carry the loss of what we were before, yes, but without lingering in grief. We are not without resources. I will invent. We have no other choice. We will absolutely have to cast off nostalgia, cast off regrets, and most of all cast off all comparisons between the before and now if we want to find the new acts we can offer to the tribe.

THURSDAY, APRIL 16, DAY 31

I can still remember very clearly the sadness I felt when Truman Burbank, the main character in the film *The Truman Show*, played by Jim Carrey, raises his hand to what he thinks is the sky and discovers, to his despair, that sky is in fact a canvas painted blue. Perhaps, for the same reasons, we shouldn't be too surprised if, contrary to what we might have imagined, with a first lifting of the lockdown carved in concrete for May 11, we might feel a certain sadness, a kind of inconsolable sorrow, and we might feel every bit as distressed as Truman Burbank. Because instinctually we know what a real horizon is, we know that a horizon brings transparency and light, while that of May 11 resembles a razor blade more than a junction between sky and sea. And while the confinement is oppressive, its end seems even more terrible because we realize it might shatter us. Perhaps because the coming of this date of May 11 will usher in a period more anxious than the framework where the lockdown, as suffocating and unbearable as it is, has held us prisoner. This framework being our own, we have the feeling we still have some control over our life in that its organization, within the circle we are granted, can be done at our convenience. The end of this framework, the erasure of its lines, the removal of its limits, instead of the relief we hoped for, brings the feeling that all these things will escape us and we will once again be at the mercy of a world in which we have less and less confidence. For after a month of being reminded that others are potential threats and that we ourselves are potential threats for others, to resume spending time with these others cannot fail to arouse a certain uneasiness. If the lockdown teaches us to discover who we are, if it becomes a chemical experiment that reveals love and lack of love, capacity and incapacity, violence and tenderness, courage and terror, it will not, however, have taught us much about living with others. Undoubtedly because before, we lived more side by side than together with others. For centuries now we have no longer believed in the spirit of the agora. Although these reasons are, to a certain extent, relevant in explaining these incomprehensible worries and sadness, although some of us recognize ourselves in this observation, there are certainly even deeper reasons that nurture these feelings of loss and sorrow. Many people are on the verge of tears without knowing why, many are filled with an immense anger, many feel great tension in their bodies without finding the words to express it. Once upon a time, there was a world that began to feel great pain in the phantom limb amputated a very long time ago. The amputation took place before the world's birth, but from one generation to the next, it was transmitted. Although we are still, in some way or another, aware of this wound, we can no longer remember what was removed from us, we no longer know what this phantom limb was, we no longer know what we are lacking. "Lack of money," some say, and they begin to pace back and forth in their glass cages, because no kingdom belongs to them; "lack of means," others will say from their windows, and they no longer even have enough tears to cry, but caught in their throats is the plaintive bird that shrieks its lament at the death of spring; "lack of space," shout many others (and they must be heard), for the sky has been robbed from them; "lack of truth, lack of consideration, lack of coherence," say those hungry for justice who feel they were tricked, but who still has the patience to listen to them? When, on the lower levels, the most violent silently throw their children out the windows, beat their heads on the sills of words, swallow alphabets, eviscerate the people they love, those to whom the kingdom of words brutally slammed shut, like old Hecuba, former queen of Troy who, driven mad by the sight of her last daughter eviscerated by the Greeks, turning towards the army to spew her hatred and call her curses down on them, was suddenly deprived of all language, and finding only a terrifying howl caught in her throat, began to bark because the words to speak her loss had dissolved in the acid of humiliation and impotence. Still others, behind words too cleverly mastered, claim they are lacking nothing, "We lack nothing," when they don't dare, in fact, say the lack of love, the lack of tenderness, the lack of sex, the lack of power, they can no longer sleep and the world of dreams has abandoned them. As for the person who tries to say her truth, "I am lazy but have had to slave all my life," that person will be greeted with laughs and jeers. Even children have forgotten what they are lacking, but children have an insatiable thirst for the infinite, and words come easily. Hour after hour, instant after instant, they say what is lacking, their lack of cellphones, tablets, computers, their lack of clothes, shoes, brand names, their lack of social media! Woe unto anyone who dares speak to them of poetry. They'll subvert the weapon of poetry to retort, "No! Shut your trap, asshole! Never speak to me again about poetry if you don't want me to chop off your head and shit on your body! I don't give a damn about your poetry, I know it all too well, your poetry, mumbled-jumbled on school stages, don't talk to me about depth or I'll eviscerate you like the cat eviscerates the mouse to enjoy its agony! I want to be superficial! I don't want to work more to earn more. I don't give a shit about your rhetoric. I want my music, my adidas, my Nikes, and I want to join the race for bargains. And Nutella. Nutella every morning! I don't need your depth, you old fogey, the most beautiful landscapes are found on the back of my cereal box! Chocapic, Honey Pops, Coco Pops, Frosties, Special K, Rice Krispies, Kellogg's Extra Buds, Nesquik, Froot Loops, Corn Flakes, Super Fibre, Make-You-Shit Fibre, Diarrhea Fibre, Shit Loops, Caca Frosties, Caca Krispies, PeepeeKrap! Don't talk to me about depth when soon you won't be ashamed to tell me about the recession, when soon you won't be ashamed to tell me we have to tighten our belts! How can you still, Daddy, hear the word *depth* when fifteen seconds later you're told: 'Go to work, go to school, study, cheat, don't cheat, smoke, don't smoke, use a rubber, don't use a rubber, fuck, suck, screw up the ass, wash your hands, spread your legs, lick, lick better, cough, don't cough, shut your mouth, be efficient, be productive!!' I'm craving, but I sure don't crave your antioxidant, organic, vegan, certified happiness. Everywhere you go, you hear:

Today it's her, tomorrow it's you,
Work is health,
The Visa card, those who have it use it,
Just do it,
Because I feel like it,
What else?
McDonald's: I'm lovin' it,
The future belongs to those who build it,
Bet on yourself,
Bounty: the Quicker Picker Upper,
Together we can do it all,
The bank you want to recommend,
Make love, not walls,
The snack that smiles back,
America runs on Dunkin',
Gillette: Male perfection,
Life is great for big and small,
Now and always Nutella, Nutella every morning!
You tell us:
Big tits!
You tell us:
Hand job
Blowjob
Cum swallowing
Cum shot

Facial
Teen
Ass
Doggy
Anal
Big cock
Bimbo
You tell us:
Amateur
You tell us:
Orgies
You say:
Fist-fucking
Tit-fucking
Ass-fucked
Ass to mouth
Black
Black hair
Asian
Arab
College
Incest
Old
Mom and son
Dad and girl
Girl and dog
Deepthroat
Doctor
MILF
Mom
Nerds
Fuck me, what a nice dick, I'm coming, I'm coming, cum, cum, on my face, on my ass, Who is she? Who is he? Oh god, oh yes!!
Performance über alles!! Performance über alles!!

Lack of this, lack of that. A screaming lack of something everywhere you look. And it seems that lack will once again define our horizon on May 11! Is it any wonder that desperate, like Truman Burbank, we raise a hand to the painted blue paper sky when we thought the sky was the sky? Marching to the tune of everything we lack. We are lacking some obscure object we can no longer call by name that's hiding in the shadows, refusing to be seen.

That's it.

We are lacking what we no longer believe in. Prisoners of this contradiction, we go round in circles, obsessed by our finiteness. And the first to dare remind us of the immense love of the universe will be a lone voice crying in the wilderness. And yet, what we lack is right here. Within reach. "Test, test, test," begged Tedros Adhanom Ghebreyesus, director-general of the World Health Organization. And what will we beg? What if, in the same unflappable tone, instead of saying, "Test, test, test," we said, "Bond, bond, bond," would the politicians hear us and do everything to reinvent a policy that promotes bonds? Then realizing that the supply of bonds is insufficient, would they place countless orders to re-establish bonds between us? Would they, as they so grandly did for protective masks on the landing strips of airports, invest millions and fight to steal the supply of bonds from other countries? France discovered that, crazy as it seems, an important supply of masks had been discarded several years ago, and that remains a source of indignation and scandal. When did we discard our supply of bonds, thinking we no longer needed them? Believing that our society, having reached the pinnacle of technological civilization, could create bonds at a lower price, virtual and efficient, replacing language with manufactured products. In doing that, we discarded much of what connected us. And now, on May 11, we will have to leave home and reconnect with others. Who could feel sad at the prospect of reconnecting? Who, if forgotten on the planet Mars after everyone left in the rocket without him, on Mars from whose skies the earth appears as small as a pinhead, who, abandoned alone there in the panic and fright of that solitude, wouldn't feel immense joy, crazy joy, when on the orange horizon, not of May 11 but of the Martian sky, they suddenly spotted the silhouette of their worst enemy? Who wouldn't start to run, tears in their eyes, screaming like mad, running towards the person whom, on earth, they had loathed their entire life? Who wouldn't feel rescued from being alone? Wouldn't any hatred be forgotten in the solidarity of that instant of great fragility? Now what must we do to feel such joy? How can we reweave the bonds between us which would, in both the smallest details and in vast political movements, make us feel a crazy desire to get up every morning and leave our homes?

FRIDAY, APRIL 17, DAY 32

I have the rare good fortune of having a Japanese friend who, in addition to managing quite well in French, speaks Greek fluently. So well in fact, he masters the nuances so well that he could easily be taken for one of the sons of Zeus who, among his thousand and one infidelities to Hera, his legitimate wife, is said to have had an adulterous relationship with Amaterasu, the Japanese goddess of the sun, a relationship which could have given birth – I can see no other explanation – to this boy, today one of my dear friends. Anyone who observes him will think the gods have something to do with his existence, despite the fact that he constantly shaves his head and wears clothes too long and too big for him, and he looks more like a little gang leader from the projects than the son of Zeus. But, Japanese to his fingertips, he was born into a Tokyo family in a working-class neighbourhood of the capital, and he grew up in the public baths which to this day belong to his parents. We met in the most cinematographic of circumstances, one day when I was playing the wise guy for a show in which I wanted to project a video in which I would perform a drowning. Well, the truth is, during this film shoot, not knowing how to swim, I did almost drown for real. We were on the island of Lemnos, off the coast of Turkey, not far from the ruins of Troy; Lemnos, where the Greek armies, led by Agamemnon, had stopped before the great battle to offer prayers and libations to the gods; Lemnos, where Philoctetes, one of the greatest Greek heroes, was bitten on his leg by a snake. Feeling that I was called, even chosen by this ancient world for which I have a deep love, I convinced myself that, like a second-rate Jean-Daniel Pollett, I absolutely had to do it all myself. So there I was, attempting to film myself drowning. I must admit I found myself very dashing, very romantic, burning with the inner fire of adventure. A clandestine operation, without having requested authorization from the island's administration, I had positioned my camera at the end of a steep, rocky jetty in such a way that it seemed to me, after falling into the water, I could remain within the frame while I simulated my drowning. A tar-black sky pressed down on the surface of the sea. The sea itself was cloudy, thick with cloying shadows, and great purple eruptions crashing all around, and the wind, released from a painting by Turner, vehemently whipped everything within reach. The entire world, from east to west, seemed to be having a seizure – waves, rocks, horizon, everything was falling apart. I had taken the precaution of choosing a place sheltered from this fury, a little cove where the waves were a bit less violent. When an imbecile gets an idea into his head, all the forces of Mount Olympus are incapable of changing his mind. That is undoubtedly why we mortals remain an enigma in the eyes of the gods, and if they have not yet erased us from the face of the earth, it is without a doubt because of this madness, this excess that is ours, which they both detest and envy. What I had to do, however, was simple. Jump into the water and come back up. More than the state of the sea, about to unleash its storm, the cold frightened me. It was the month of January and with the wind chill, the temperature was about zero degrees. Furthermore, I don't like water, good weather, bad weather, I don't like the water. I don't like the sea, I don't like to go swimming, be it in a river, a brook, a stream, a pool, a bathtub. I am a cat. Imagine my apprehension. I was wearing two pairs of pants, two diving outfits, and three pairs of socks. I set the camera focus, I approached the edge of the jetty, I made my way over several rocks to reach the place where all I had to do was jump. For a second I wondered whether this was reasonable, before calling myself a chicken. If I had been more attentive, I undoubtedly would have heard, from the heights of Mount

Olympus, the gasp of the gods, Zeus, Athena, Apollo, Arte-
mis, Hera, Hermes, Aphrodite, and the whole gang, stupefied,
glued to their screens, subjugated by my performance, and
Poseidon, pensive, scratching his cheek with his trident, wondering what he was going to do with this strange mortal.
Retrospectively, I believe I heard them saying to themselves,
"Who is this idiot?" And Athena urging her uncle, master of
the seas, to have no pity on me, while Aphrodite, caressing
his beard, raising her hand to her mouth, was begging him
to give this fool a chance, if only as a reward for the enter-
taining moment I was offering them. Perhaps Poseidon went
so far as to point out the fury of the waves and insisted that
he was doing everything possible to make me listen to reason,
but at that moment, deaf to all that, listening only to my
courage, I threw myself into the water. And the sea took me.
Ah! the sensation of pure terror when I felt it seize me as
suddenly as a toad swallows an insect with a flick of the
tongue. I was caught in the palm of the waves, an autumn
leaf carried off in a gust of wind, suddenly I was nothing but
a trinket tossing, tumbling, rolling at the mercy of the currents. I lost all my bearings, had no sense of up or down, the
shore or the open sea, and gasping, choking, sputtering,
I knew my time had come. It was a Minotaur moment, I'd
say, where in the seconds I had left to live and in the primitive
agitation thrashing inside me, one or two faces appeared, the
essence of my existence. And in that moment, I can bear
witness, I understand how clearly we become aware of living
the last seconds of our life, and in the grip of those last
moments, like a lightning bolt slashing the sky of our brain,
the question of our happiness appears. Were you happy? Are
you leaving in peace? This awareness has the advantage of
making time slow down and triggering a great panic. "It's
not true, it's not true, it's not true, it's not true!" Then very
quickly, somehow, from some absolutely incomprehensible
source, an insane strength wells up inside us, like a flash, not
to fight death but, on the contrary, to console waning life.

"Calm down, stop, stop panicking, stop! You're going to die, it doesn't matter, calm down and don't waste these last seconds!" Obviously it's not that precise, but it resembles a power of acceptance we didn't know we possessed. A power that speeds us closer to the desire to end the agony, to reach the goal of all this and to finally know what comes after and to belong to this wholeness that will continue with us, but in another way, a totally different way. Over the course of these few seconds, I felt a kind of excitement, thinking that I would finally know. That, finally, I too would participate. And in jumbled fragments, I believe I remembered these lines from Shakespeare: "to take arms against a sea of troubles / And by opposing end them" – without knowing whether they came from *Hamlet* or *Othello*, and I heard, I believe, my mother's voice telling me to vacuum the room and pay attention to the corners, I saw the path that led from the house to the mountain and the forest where I used to play, I even think I saw the dog from Tarkovsky's *Stalker* and the red-and-black cover of the paperback edition of Kafka's *Metamorphosis*. All that at once, but with dizzying precision. I almost forgot I was dying. Then remembering again, seized from head to toe by the last spasms of my terrified heart, I felt the sharp bite of sorrow at the thought that I would not see my children grow up and that this marvellous life was about to end. Again I tried to struggle, although rationally I knew it was useless to hope for anything. "You don't know how to swim, the sea is stormy, and you are drowning, like thousands and thousands of migrants drown every day along these same Greek shores, and no one makes a fuss about it. Why make such a big deal of your drowning? So calm down and accept." It was at that very moment, I think, that a sense of great resilience invaded my mind and I was no longer afraid of anything, and just as drowning was about to end my life came the conviction, the certainty that no matter what happens, no matter how one dies, beyond the moment of terror, beyond the surprise, beyond any regrets, something inside us is standing guard, prepared to spring into action to reassure us and ensure that we can die in peace. I began to have faith in death and started to accept placing myself in its care. It was almost a sensation of joy, an intense feeling of life that simply accepts its end. And I was accepting. At last, I was accepting. For the first time in my life, I knew how, I could almost easily accept what was happening to me, something I had always failed to do. I had, I believe, ceased to struggle for a moment, when I felt a force pulling me and in the blurred consciousness that followed, I believed that my body had gotten caught on a rock. My arm was caught between my chest and my throat. The idea of dying strangled by myself seemed grotesque to me as I was drowning. I even had time to reflect that, truly, one is never satisfied, as if my arm in that position was preventing me from dying peacefully. I wanted to escape its embrace, I wanted to change its position, when I realized that this arm I was fighting with, I was holding it in my own two hands! It was absurd, where did my third arm come from? Logically, it couldn't be mine! Immediately the idea that I was no longer alone, that someone was there, someone was there determined to save me, came over me. For a fraction of a second, I confess I was almost disappointed – "Oh, no! I almost made it!" – something along those lines, and then common sense, the desire to live, hope, took over and made me think, "No, c'mon, help him, help him, you fool, instead of acting like dead weight, help him!" and I held on, I held on and I did what I could, I struggled, until I passed out completely. The memories are confused to this day, but when I remember the scenes that followed, the first one I remember, because it is so very clear, begins when, sitting facing this Japanese man, I see his round, hilarious face. He was speaking to me in French, telling me how he had seen me jump into the sea and how he had jumped in after me. I remember him smiling from ear to ear, happy to see me there, alive, with him, then laughing so hard he was crying as I told him, no, I wasn't trying to commit suicide, it had absolutely nothing to do with suicide, but that I wanted to capture some images for my artistic schemes and that, despite not knowing how to swim, I thought I had been careful. In the wake of that laughter, we became friends.

This Japanese friend, in addition to many other advantages, is able to answer any question related to the Greek etymology of French words. Whenever I wonder, I send him a text message. That is how, one day when I asked him whether the word *catastrophe* was related to the poetic *strophe* (stanza) in Racine's verses, he answered, yes of course, bravo for my perspicacity (in addition to being Japanese and speaking French and Greek, he is always kind enough to raise my spirits with hearty encouragement), and he proceeded to explain that, very specifically, these two words, *catastrophe* and *strophe*, had the same root:

"*Strophe*, from the Greek noun *strophē* στροφή, which by extension means **curve** or **turn**. And *cata-*, from the Greek preposition *kata* κατά, which means **over**, as in *overlook*, **to be above, greater**, as in *overturn*. So you see, to sum up, we can translate, if you wish, uhh … the idea of a *catastrophe* as being **a big turn, a shift**. *Catastrophe*, as if we were saying **a big shift**."

"Ah, I see," I tell him, "so in Greece today, for example, if I take a taxi, I can simply tell the driver, 'You can take the first *strophe* on the left, then continue on straight ahead and make sure you don't miss the *catastrophe* as we leave the village."

"If you wish, sure. I'm not sure you'll reach your destination, but you can say that, yes, you can say that."

I couldn't believe it. The big turn. Perhaps we are now in the big turn, at the tip of the hairpin turn. The pandemic as a turn at the end of the road, a *strophe*, a stanza, a hemistich maybe, an alexandrine, in any case, an act after which something will overturn us, a virus, death, disappearance, a big turn. But where will it lead us? Now tell me, my beloved Japanese friend, what does *cataclysm* mean?

"Well, you see, *cataclysm* is more relevant to you, with your drowning, because *kataclusmos* κατακλυσμός evokes the liquid element. You find the root in *clyster*, **enema**, for example, cleansing, the act of **washing. To wet, to soak.** *Clysm*, *cata-clysm*, **the big washing. The big cleaning.** And by extension, **the flood. Flooding.** The story of Noah is the inaugural cataclysm."

There you have it: this unique friend I can call upon night and day, regardless of the different time zones between us. And tonight, having decided at last to dive into reading the Apocalypse, hoping to understand whether what we are going through is more like a "catastrophe," a "cataclysm," or an "apocalypse," I asked him what this last word means, how, given his extremely Eastern turn of mind, as someone born of people who experienced two atomic bombs, for whom these words must have a very real and particular resonance, how does he perceive that word, *apocalypse*, ἀποκάλυψις.

"It is quite literally the **un-veiling.** *Apo-* ἀπο-, **un-**; ἀποκάλυψις, **veiling.** In other words, the **revelation.** Revelation as the demonstration of what had been hidden, dissimulated. The negative connotation the word has acquired in contemporary language that makes it synonymous with an absolute, end-of-the-world catastrophe is merely a consequence of the terrifying content of the biblical Apocalypse and its revelations, whereas the word itself is perfectly positive in its etymology, it's simply **a revealing, an unveiling** and not necessarily a catastrophe intended to bring on the end of the world. In modern Greek, you see, any revelation, even neighbourhood gossip, is called an ἀποκάλυψη. I can't begin to tell you the number of 'apocalypses' printed every day in the Greek equivalents of *Paris Match*, *Voici*, and *Gala*, reporting that so-and-so is going out with so-and-so, or that so-and-so has had plastic surgery."

"No! Are you saying that when, every day, we learn what we learn about Johnny Hallyday's life and death, these are 'apocalypses'!!!?"

"Absolutely!"

"I have no more questions for you."

Apocalypse. Apocalypse as a revelation, an unveiling. Perhaps this is the path that can lead me to the place where this virus is at work inside us. It reveals so much about us. Apocalypse, then, in its most powerful sense, far from the weight of the catastrophes and the cataclysms. And then, without intending to, I thought about Ulysses prisoner on the goddess's island, and immediately the name of Calypso had a difference resonance. Without the *apo-*. **Un-**veiling without the **un-**. The veil. Calypso, the one who veils, the dissimulator. The sudden connection between these two words that I had never made left me speechless, my conviction was so strong that we were, like Homer's hero, prisoners of a goddess on a shore and nostalgic for something we can no longer see, but something of which we feel, today more than ever, the cruel lack.

MONDAY, APRIL 20, DAY 35

Today I'm going to read slowly. My window washing was so intense, the glass on the sliding door overlooking the yard was so clean, that thinking it was still open, I hit my head so hard I fainted. When I regained consciousness, my daughter asked what had come over me. I told her that I simply hadn't seen the door. She took this as proof that doing things well wasn't always good. Unwilling to engage in a Socratic dialogue with a teenager using irony to denigrate paternal authority, I lay there musing on the ways our convictions about things can lead us to collide with their exact opposite. I thought it was open; it was closed. Hadn't that happened to me more than once on other subjects? Suddenly I felt very depressed, stupid, useless, in short, a twit. I regretted my zealous cleaning binge. What a dumb idea, washing windows on a Sunday morning! There's always a trap in our best intentions, a blind spot. When driving, there are two ways to see what's hiding in the blind spot. The first is to turn to look through the side windows in the back of the car. The second is to change speed, accelerate or slow down, while checking the rear-view mirror. But as efficient as these ways might be, neither eliminates the blind spot; they both simply change its location. There is still a blind spot. That's true of cars and of human beings, too. Be it relative to our knowledge of the world or to that of those around us, it's always there, a blind spot, lurking in the shadows, and although they are always dangerous, no blind spot is as dangerous as the one we all have about ourselves. Given that blind spot, it's easy to understand the importance of the reminder inscribed on the porch of the Temple of Apollo at Delphi that greeted every visitor who came to consult the oracle: "Know thyself." In other words: "You, mortal, remember that you do not have the peripheral vision of the gods. A blind spot is always lying in wait. Be careful about what you claim about yourself, be careful about what you claim about others. Use your rear-view mirror, accelerate, slow down, force yourself to turn around, take a three-quarters look behind you, don't get stuck in one point of view, neither about others nor yourself, and most of all, avoid getting zealous about anything related to housekeeping." Ever since the sixth century BCE, when the temple at Delphi was presumably built, human beings have dreaded the thought of losing the gift of clairvoyance and, although it has lost some of its sacredness, the danger persists to this day. The motto "Know thyself" could be translated today by this truth that none of my contemporaries would refute: "They who are becoming old assholes don't know that they're becoming old assholes." Effectively, this pathology is not painful, the victims are convinced that they still have an open-minded, generous, empathetic, intelligent view of the world. No old asshole wants to be one, and yet many become just that, unbeknownst to themselves. This ignorance is undoubtedly a result of the anaesthesia brought on by obstinate singlemindedness, the stubborn determination to always frame things in the same way, to defend the same view at all costs. This singlemindedness cancels the capacity to see the overly clean glass and to question oneself (given the illusion that one is always questioning oneself). This is a pernicious sickness, the most pernicious of all, very often asymptomatic for the person suffering from it. The old asshole has no idea. He is aware of nothing, sees nothing, is always confident about everything he does. I must confess now that becoming a victim of this pathology terrifies me more than most things, including the virus. Precautions can be taken and I promised myself, after my head-on collision with the pane of glass this morning, to practise them more rigorously: to question myself the way I wash my hands, four times a day; look into the gaze of others, from less than a metre away, and try to see in the eyes of others what others observe in me that I cannot see; know that it can happen to me any day, that it doesn't just happen to others, it can happen to me and there is no test, serological or other, capable of reassuring me. No vaccine has been found, no point in testing it on animals, it is a pathology that only affects humans. And as for herd immunity, although it might have been reached given the number of cases among us, it has been proven that it doesn't protect anyone. Stupidity continues to spread. We cannot let down our guard. And if we have caught the sickness, spouting, in the kind of moment of inattention that can strike anyone, an incalculable number of idiotic ideas, and if, afterwards, we were able to recover thanks to an immense effort of self-questioning, well, whatever we do, we shouldn't believe we are immune. There is no antibody that can protect us from obtuseness. The blind spot in each one of us isn't fixed. It's like quicksand, constantly appearing and disappearing. It's invisible and unpredictable. We are always blind to something. There is always a blind spot. The transparency of the glass was simply one among many in my mishap this morning. What do I fail to see about myself? Can you tell me without making me faint in fear? And how to hear it in any case? After the tenth plague descended upon Egypt, the pharaoh, who'd had several occasions to see and hear what he should have seen and heard, obstinately continued his stubborn course and refused to let the Hebrew people go. In Exodus 10:7, before darkness fell over the land, there is the desperate servants' plea to the pharaoh: "Let the men go ... Knowest thou not yet that Egypt is destroyed?" But Pharaoh doesn't see it, as enormous as it was, he doesn't see it, he's incapable of seeing it; he doesn't see it, either because the glass is too clean or because he stubbornly refuses to turn his head to look out the rear side windows, he refuses to make the effort, refuses to accelerate or to slow down, obstinately continuing to see what he'd been seeing so far. And Egypt was lost with the sea closing over his warriors. Like the woman from

Québec, visiting the Theresienstadt concentration camp in the Czech Republic as a tourist in the summer of 2004, who after a few hasty, bored glances at the children's drawings conserved in what is now a museum that documents the deportation of European Jews, as I was standing close by, and no doubt assuming I wouldn't understand, exclaimed to her companion: "This is pretty boring, right? I prefer Auschwitz." She preferred Auschwitz, because in Auschwitz, as she proceeded to tell her companion: "You know, there were the ovens, and the hair, and that was interesting. Here there's nothing but kids' drawings." Is that what prompted Kafka to write one of his most powerful aphorisms? "In the struggle between yourself and the world, side with the world." Was it because, with his prophetic sensitivity, he had heard both the words of the pharaoh and foreseen those of the Québec tourist, and wishing to expose this blindness, he wrote those few words? "In the struggle between yourself and the world, side with the world." What I hear in this sentence is an invitation to be careful, to practise caution, given that, in terms of vision, I am confronted by the greatest mystery. What, in fact, do we see? From what angle are we looking? What do we think we see? And what can we see from our houses? Five weeks in the thrall of my computer screen, unable to see anything of the outside world, but surprisingly every time I turned my head to look out the window, I seemed to notice something else, to feel something about the world, something clearer, precisely because I was inside and not outside, and I was looking at the world from inside. I was looking at the world from inside. It took me a while to grasp the meaning of this intuition. How could I, looking out my window, see more than I saw watching the stream of live coverage posted by major newspapers on the internet, or reading the scholarly articles which had the advantage of keeping me informed? Why do I feel I can learn more by going outside for a few minutes? But to learn what? Why do I feel this desire to free myself of all that? What is this voice that seems to be telling me, "What are you hoping to learn? What do you want to know, more than what you already know about this situation?" A partial answer came to me on this Sunday when, reeling under the weight of an indescribable pressure directed at me by a young six-and-a-half-year-old padawan, I gave in, and weakness, baseness, surrender, the Force wasn't with me, I set up the video projector to watch *Revenge of the Sith*, the third episode in the *Star Wars* saga. This was no mean feat, since there are no curtains or blinds on the windows and before we could sit down for the film, in order to see something, I had to block the light with sheets and some wood panels. "It's weird that we have to be in the dark to see something," said the young padawan at my side, but even then, prey to obtuseness again, I didn't really hear what he had just said. I didn't understand. And we started to watch the film. I knew it well, having already seen it several times, but watching it in the company of a child who discovers, to his amazement, that the little boy he became attached to in episode 1 was none other than this ruthless man who assassinates the entire crew of Jedi in episode 3 made me perceive the film differently and, most of all, it allowed me to see one of the most beautiful scenes in a new light and to grasp its meaning in a stunning way. It must be said that this moment, which happens in the final minutes of the film, is a cinematographic image dear to the hearts of many *Star Wars* fans. Bathed in macabre light, surrounded by the glacial emanations of a sterile space the walls of which fade into darkness, a darkness that evokes the side of the Force he has slipped into, Anakin Skywalker is about to seal his fate. Stretched out on a circular table, a veritable metallic rose window around which surgical droids are busily transforming his calcined body, whose arms and legs have been amputated, suddenly Anakin emerges from his chrysalis and becomes Darth Vader, soon to achieve, along with Reverend Harry Powell in *The Night of the Hunter*, Norman Bates in *Psycho*, and Frank in *Once upon a Time in the West*, the truly mythical status of one of the most memorable bad guys in the popular movies of the twentieth century. In this narratively powerful scene, one shot stands out among all the others. In addition to its great simplicity and beauty, this single shot offers the fans of George Lucas's saga a glimpse into the interior of Darth Vader's legendary mask. The mystery of all mysteries for the past thirty years! Anakin, his face burned, opens his eyes and stares at this mask that will confine him forever. Shot from a subjective angle, this image, lasting four seconds, allows us to see what Darth Vader sees, it's a shot that takes us inside Darth Vader's vision. We become him, and having access to his vision, piercing the enigma of his vision, understanding his suffering, through this shared vision, we become Darth Vader, we become the bad guy, and for one second we hate the Jedi and wish for their extermination. There are, therefore, no monsters, there are only human beings. This black, unexpressive, metallic face, that I had always found opaque and until then identified with the character of the bad guy, is humanized by this shot. Darth Vader is no longer simply a mask, he has become someone. In other words there is someone locked up inside, someone who can see from within. Someone on the inside looking at the outside. No one can dispute that fact that to truly appreciate the beauty of rose windows, they must be contemplated from the inside. From the inside the stone lacework appears in all its delicacy enhanced by the addition of the stained glass, vibrating in the rays of sunshine like a harp beneath the musician's fingers, by the play of colours and hues, revealing the perfect circles that enclose them, set in the nave of cathedrals, and called rose windows because they evoke the shape of the flower. We have to be inside the body of the cathedral to see, we have to be inside the dark, with the invincible sun outside, to appreciate the beauty of roses in all their splendour. Something in this metamorphosis made me stand up, as if struck by a supernatural revelation. We have to be inside to see! In a book on architecture I borrowed from my local library,

I admired the marvellous roses in Notre-Dame Cathedral and in Chartres Cathedral. The most beautiful rose windows were conceived in the thirteenth century. Subdivided into many medallions placed in several concentric circles, the rose in the nave of Notre-Dame measures more than twelve metres in diameter. The medallions allow us to see life on earth from a different point of view, they tell the story of the battle between positive and negative values, while each circle evokes in turn the vectors that shape daily life, the seasons, work in the fields, and all of this using both religious and pagan symbols, in colours of indescribable beauty. Although all the medallions are different, it is their cohesion and the design of the circles that shape this rose. It is a palimpsest of different images, a mosaic composed of the contradictions in our lives. If this is how rose windows are, it's because our minds are like that, too, and these cathedral roses were undoubtedly conceived this way to allow us to see how the magma of ideas acts in them. Imagining my mind like a rose window, suddenly I saw in it a beauty, a simplicity, and what I considered dispersion was revealed as a multiplicity. Three concentric circles occupied the field of my thoughts. First of all, the present: all the issues related to the current day. The children, how to occupy them, how to teach them, food, errands, and the daily routine, and the moments of silence, writing, its place, the emptiness during walks and sleepless nights. The concern for those dear to us, the fatigue, the media, the news – all of that like so many medallions set in the circle of the present. Then there was the circle of the past: the memory of the war in Lebanon which is constantly revived by this confinement, the death of those close to us, often departed too soon, the dispersion of family members, the separation from friends, but also the memory of marvellous moments, the ice-cold glass of rose water that awaited me when I returned from my walks during the heatwaves in the summer, the years of training at the theatre school in Canada, in Montréal, the people I met there, the friendships, the loves, and the shows, the opening nights, the euphoric moments and the artistic adventures that remain like flashes of eternity, all that, each memory a medallion in the circle of the past. And then there was the circle of the future, and the questions that obsess me as we approach the day of May 11: what will become of the theatre, the shows, the casts and crews. And how will we be able to mount shows without touching each other, without hugging each other, for theatre is made of contact and embraces in a space where the actors, whether in rehearsal or performance, sweat, spit, sputter, and grapple with each other often? And then imagining the children of today as the adults of tomorrow. Trying to cancel the thought that suggests that all this, this virus, is only the sign of greater disasters yet to come. And this, too, each thought, each idea, was a separate medallion in the circle of the future, the whole, present, past, and future, composing the immense rose window of my mind. And if a rose is only visible from the inside, if, to contemplate it, one has to be confined, what was the nature of the light that filled my mind, revealing, with its powerful illumination, the medallions and the circles of this rose? Then I recalled the comment of the young padawan: "It's weird that it has to be dark to see something." It's true that as I was making the room dark, I realized that the only light that guided me over the past five weeks was the cold bitter light shed by this virus and confinement. Unable to see things, present, past, or future, other than in the light of these circumstances, this light revealed a rose that has become my blind spot which I must at all costs escape if I want to avoid being trapped like the pharaoh. That's when I thought of all the writing projects lying dormant in me for the past five weeks, neglected since the beginning of the lockdown. And I saw that they no longer occupy spaces in the circles of my mind. I thought about the silence I miss and I also thought about the need to make a wild leap at a moment I hadn't been able to foresee. When I began writing this journal, I rejected the idea of any preparation in advance and I always dove into writing without knowing where it would take me, always betting on uncertainty rather than on the principle of precaution which would have entailed preparation and making plans. And now, as I write what I am writing today, about the pharaoh, about the tourist from Québec, about myself, thinking of Kafka's aphorism and following the thread of my sensations, I reach, the first to be surprised, through the magic of all these things combined together, the conclusion that this must come to an end. Writing this journal must come to an end. Not because I am incapable of continuing, on the contrary, but precisely because it has become easier for me to continue than to stop. Roses remain opaque when viewed from outside. They reveal only their stone enclosure and the murkiness of stained glass. To be seen, they must be viewed from inside. This conclusion is obvious and reminds me how knowing how to end should never depend upon a date imposed by others, not even when it's the President of the République. We write until a certain signal, an epiphany as incomprehensible as it is unexpected, makes itself heard. Now that the end of the lockdown is approaching, I will end this journal here. I will continue to write, but in silence.

A SUBLIMATION

In an ironic twist of fate, I find myself correcting the proofs of these texts written during the lockdown last spring, just as we enter another lockdown. Proofs, the publisher's trial run, in this case, proof of the trials and tribulations of the first lockdown as we enter the second. Proofs vs. proof. Confinement and re-confinement. Almost the same words, but the plural -s and the prefix *re-* make all the difference as we teeter on the edge of trials to come.

While a certain solidarity emerged at the beginning of the pandemic, bringing humans together, a kind of brutality has entered relationships this autumn. A brutality that pits the health of the economy against the interests of public health, since the economy requires connections, exchanges, and close collaboration, while the battle with the virus demands solitude, separation, and distancing. In this conflict, the spirit that lives in every human being has everything to lose. Called upon to determine what is essential in their view, day after day, societies see dreams and utopias disintegrate. Overwhelmed, democratic governments have no choice but to use their power to impose the new norms of our era and to save physical and economic health.

Sadness resurfaces. Youth, although unable to express it, experience a deep sense of injustice, our living spaces shrink, the sky loses its sharpness in the haze of the general mood. Lucky are the people who, impervious to this collective melancholy, don't see their inner boundaries collide and still manage to know where they stand. Landscapes are eroded, humidity oppresses everything, weighs upon everything, erases clarity like in an overexposed photograph where the coarse grain blurs the shapes and the lines. With this loss of real structure, as if through a blotter, we see traces of a world that no longer exists, yet we cling to it. A smudged drawing never regains its initial outline.

"What's the matter with you?" asks an attentive friend.

"I don't know."

How to answer when you can hardly manage to differentiate between trees and their shadows, faces and their reflections, and between words and words. We cross streets and boulevards with the impression of living, not inside out, but truly upside down. But, we are constantly asking ourselves, upside down from what? And within this crippled daily existence, we all do the best we can and we struggle to keep our lives afloat. This life seems so absurd and so precious. We do what we have to do, although it makes no sense at all. The limited leeway of our lives, within which and thanks to which we managed to escape the vicissitudes of existence, that leeway is more limited than ever. With no more reason for being than to continue being, to be becomes an anatomical injunction: stay alive. Re-become a reproductive animal, eating and defecating.

And yet! In tasting the apple in the Garden of Eden, we became aware that it wasn't enough to live just to live, being alive wasn't enough to feel alive. Who cares about paradise! It's better to be damned and to live joyously in pain and affliction than to remain deprived of all knowledge, subjected to sanctimonious joy.

The shrinking of this leeway, the leeway that enables us to be the artists of our own lives, that makes so many refugees flee their homes in the hope of finding possibilities elsewhere, that inspires courage in the youth of every generation and drives prisoners to plot escape, this leeway without which existence would be reduced to the fulfillment of basic needs in no way equal to the insatiable thirst for the infinite that lives in the heart of each and every one of us, the shrinking of that leeway is the cause of our bewilderment. If meaning is a horizon, today its line has slipped from its groove and having lost what extended it from west to east, that line has collapsed brutally and is left twisted and tangled, winding itself around us, it has become a labyrinth. Having lost the possibility of dreaming the future, we have become prisoners of a present trying to catch its breath.

Such is life this autumn. What will it be like in the spring? What will it be like when this book reaches bookstores? What will be our state of mind when we look back in amazement at everything we once believed and everything we've lost, everything we continue to mourn.

The texts in this collection were written day after day to be recorded and posted as podcasts. They were conceived with the candid idea that no one can fight uncertainty alone. That it's easier to move ahead together. That a voice in the darkness can provide courage to those seeking it in a maze the extent of which is unknown. When will we emerge? No one can answer and once again today no one can affirm anything about the future. Within this uncertainty, each of us must carry on according to our individual capacities. Mine meant bearing witness, telling stories and tales, my brand of oral history, speaking aloud, capturing the poetry of what it means to speak out. While this diary, like all diaries, is based on real facts, events from daily life during the lockdown, it is also tinted by the fiction that emerges while writing. If writing means choosing what we wish to be a slave to, I never wanted to be a slave to reality. In fact I've never been able to say what reality is and I've always been drawn to its deformation since, as María Zambrano so brilliantly wrote, "It's not a question of moving from the possible to the real, but rather from the impossible to the true." This impossible sublimated in the true is undoubtedly the nature of "lying-true" so dear to Aragon. And it is all the more crucial when it comes to a diary. Without this shifting, there would be no infractions in poetry.

For me, writing a diary requires accepting that the essential is elsewhere, unnameable, eluding awareness. In other terms, remembering that *meanwhile* something is at work inside us. Something indifferent to what is suffocating us, like the child hidden in the bushes, playing with his shoelace. Something that doesn't need us goes on living inside us. While we are worrying, raging, complaining, while we are struggling, obsessing, despairing, while we are in the tumultuous present of our times, meanwhile, something inside us, greater than us, more powerful than us, and despite us, is at work inside us. And this something, like the outside when we are inside, is exactly that opposite that spurs us on. *Fish-self* that calls us each by name and whose shimmering scales also reflect our image. While the daily writing of this diary had the goal of bearing witness to that elusive self, its publication hopes to offer those who followed it the possibility of revisiting the moments that mattered to them. There can be many clearings, there can be many suns.

—WAJDI MOUAWAD
November 20, 2020

EDITOR'S NOTE

The texts in this collection were first recorded in French by the author and broadcast on the Théâtre national de la Colline website between March 16 and April 20, 2020; see www.colline.fr/spectacles /journal-de-confinement-de-wajdi-mouawad. Episodes are available on Spotify (open.spotify.com /show/5EelZmj9PeDLCd3DEuBSle) and Sound-Cloud (soundcloud.com/user-308301388/sets /journal-de-confinement).

SOURCES

All translations are by Linda Gaboriau unless otherwise noted. Bible quotes are from the King James version.

March 18: "Happy the one who, like Ulysses" is from "Heureux qui comme Ulysse" (written between 1553 and 1557) by Joachim du Bellay.

March 25: The quotes from Marcel Proust's *In Search of Lost Time* are from the translation by C.K. Scott Moncrieff, Terence Kilmartin, and Andreas Mayor, revised by D.J. Enright (New York: Chatto & Windus and Random House, 1981).

March 26: "Night would be eternal without the night" is from the afterword to Robert Davreu's *Au passage de l'heure*, (Paris: Éditions Corti, 2001).

"Do not go gentle into that good night" is from the poem of the same title by Dylan Thomas, *The Poems of Dylan Thomas* (New York: New Directions, 2003).

April 3: "So many poppies growing among the weeds" is from "Le pré de mai" by Philippe Jaccottet, in *Paysages avec figures absentes* (Paris: Gallimard, 1970).

April 20: "In the struggle between yourself and the world, side with the world" is from the December 8, 1917, entry in Franz Kafka's *Journal* (Paris: Grasset, 2002).

A Sublimation: "It's not a question of moving from the possible to the real" is from María Zambrano, *Philosophie et poésie*, translated from Spanish into French by Jacques Ancet (Paris: Éditions Corti, 2004).

Linda Gaboriau is an award-winning literary translator based in Montréal. Her translations of plays by Québec's most prominent playwrights have been published and produced across Canada and abroad. In her work as a literary manager and dramaturge, she has directed numerous translation residencies and international exchange projects. She is the founding director of the Banff International Literary Translation Centre. Gaboriau has won the Governor General's Award for Translation three times: in 1996 for Daniel Danis's *Stone and Ashes*, in 2010 for Wajdi Mouawad's *Forests*, and in 2019 for Wajdi Mouawad's *Birds of a Kind*. She is a member of the Order of Canada and an Officer of the Ordre national du Québec.

Over the past twenty years, **Wajdi Mouawad** has risen to fame in Canada and internationally, acclaimed for the power of his writing and the originality of his vision as a theatre director. He is the author of an epic quartet for the stage, The Blood of Promises (*Tideline*, *Scorched*, *Forests*, *Heavens*), and two novels, *Visage retrouvé* and *Anima*, which won numerous prizes. His work has been translated into more than twenty languages, and his plays have been produced around the world. In 2016 he was named artistic director of La Colline – Théâtre national in Paris.

[DAY 18]

[DAY 21]

[DAY 22]

[DAY 23]

[DAY 24]

[DAY 25]

[DAY 28]

[DAY 29]

[DAY 30]

[DAY 31]

[DAY 32]

[DAY 35]

[DAY 0]

[DAY 1]

[DAY 2]

[DAY 3]

[DAY 7]

[DAY 8]

[DAY 9]

[DAY 10]

[DAY 11]

[DAY 14]

[DAY 15]

[DAY 16]

[DAY 17]